God Will Provide

How God's Bounty Opened to Saints—
and 9 Ways It Can Open for You, Too

PATRICIA TREECE

PARACLETE PRESS
BREWSTER, MASSACHUSETTS

2013 Second printing
2011 First printing

God Will Provide: How God's Bounty Opened to Saints—and 9 Ways It Can Open for You, Too

Copyright © 2011 by Patricia Treece

ISBN 978-1-61261-045-0

Library of Congress Cataloging-in-Publication Data

Treece, Patricia.
  God will provide : how God's bounty opened to saints and 9 ways it can open for you, too / Patricia Treece.
    p. cm.
  Includes index.
  ISBN 978-1-61261-045-0 (pbk.)
    1. Spiritual life—Catholic Church. 2. Providence and government of God—Christianity. 3. Christian saints. I. Title.
  BX2350.3.T74 2011
  248.4'82—dc23   2011036835

10 9 8 7 6 5 4 3 2

Published by Paraclete Press
Brewster, Massachusetts
www.paracletepress.com

Printed in the United States of America

To all who need and want
Divine Providence
in their lives

and

to God's friend and mine
Alice Williams
whose prayers have obtained
from Divine Providence every kind of grace
and blessing for me, my family,
and countless others.

CONTENTS

A NOTE TO MY READERS

Don't be afraid to read this if you're not Catholic. The principles are universal and will work for anyone willing to give them a try. If the word *saint* seems strange, call them "God's friends." And yes, some of God's non-Catholic friends turn up here, too.

Because there are some stupendous true stories in these pages, let me assure you: anything involving a saint is taken from the authentic sources as verified by the individual's order, shrine, or my years of research into the individual's life, writings, letters, and the testimonies, often under oath, by those who knew them. The smaller number involving non-saints happened to people of the highest integrity I know personally (except for never having the honor of meeting the late founder of Habitat for Humanity, Millard Fuller) or are events I was involved in myself.

As an example of my sources, the prologue you are about to read was written from the testimony of an eyewitness, a saint's coworker and fellow Capuchin Franciscan. The Capuchin order supplied a copy of the account for my work. However, since copious footnotes scare away some readers, it was decided to put only some sources in footnotes and give others in a section entitled "Sources on the Saints," found at the back of the book. I hope this solution will promote readability for all, while without too much trouble, providing for you who need surety that I have not made up even one of this book's amazing events!

God Will Provide

The Depths of the Great
Worldwide Depression of the 1930s
St. Bonaventure Friary
Detroit, Michigan

"Father Solanus, Father Solanus!" Father Herman Buss rushes into the porter's office, where his fellow Capuchin[1] has been giving himself totally, as usual, to someone in need. "Sorry," Father Herman says as he brushes past a radiant-faced woman heading out of the office door. "There's nothing to offer the men. Not even a scrap of bread, and we've got two or three hundred waiting for the door to open."

The porter of St. Bonaventure's Friary on Mount Elliott Avenue, Father Solanus, turns serene blue eyes to Father Herman. He nods in understanding. He doesn't say, "Why tell me?" After God himself, the poor and the sick are Solanus' greatest love.

As for the sick, whether in Solanus' three posts in New York, Indiana, or here in Detroit, Michigan, there have been so many "impossible cures" through the smiling, stick-thin Capuchin's prayers that he has been charged with keeping a log of visitors'

---

1 One of three major and many smaller religious Orders that follow Christ via St. Francis of Assisi's spirituality.

prayer requests and the results. He does so gladly, knowing it is God, not he, who heals.

The poor and hungry always turn up at monasteries. Solanus has fed many a man in the friary kitchen—sometimes cheerfully setting his own simple dinner before his unknowing guest. But feeding individually will no longer do. The Depression has brought the desperately hungry out in unprecedented numbers. The Capuchins have opened a soup kitchen—although the standard meal is not soup but a meaty stick-to-your-ribs stew meant to sustain someone eating only once a day. The kitchen is down the block from the friary in a building devoted to Third Order (that is, lay, or non-ordained) Franciscans. Although no one voices this, Father Herman has no doubt that Solanus is the spiritual force behind the kitchen, that in an ongoing miracle is feeding as many as three thousand a day.

Whenever Solanus' job of porter lets him get away, he helps materially as well. This may take the form of a trip out to a farm to pick fruit a farmer offers or to help load free vegetables for those hearty stews. Wisconsin farm-bred, his brown habit's hood slung back, Solanus finds the same stores of energy for throwing sacks of potatoes onto a volunteer driver's truck that he once displayed as part of the Casey brothers' baseball team. In town he pitches the needs of the hungry to butchers, bakers, and anyone with significant food to spare.

But the day has come at last.

In spite of all Father Solanus has done, in spite of all Father Herman, assigned there full time, has done, in spite of all the volunteer lay Franciscans who cook, serve, and themselves donate, have done, the kitchen is out of food.

Father Solanus walks back with anxious Father Herman, who will never forget and later report in writing[2] what happens next. Solanus goes out to the men. He doesn't tell them he is sorry there is nothing to feed them today. He tells them truthfully, "There is no food." Then, even as some—among them men who have not eaten for several days—prepare with despairing faces to turn back toward the street, he says authoritatively in his low voice permanently scarred by childhood diphtheria, "Wait. Just wait. *God will provide.*"

Lined up are men of every stripe—the gamut of Protestants, a sprinkling of Jews, devout Catholics and Catholics in name only, and people who have nothing to do with any kind of religion. Without insistence, Solanus—whose God-given miracles go out as readily to any who ask as to his fellow Catholics—invites them to join him in prayer. Many follow along as he says the *Our Father* with its petition "Give us this day our daily bread."

Barely has the last word left his lips when a man dressed in a bakery uniform seemingly appears out of nowhere, making his way across the line of men with a huge basket of bread. One basket isn't enough for two hundred to three hundred men but no matter: as he passes into the kitchen, his voice floats back saying he's brought a truckload of foodstuffs.

Relieved and overjoyed, some men start to cry, tears glistening on whisker-stubbled cheeks.

Solanus, who sees God do astounding things day after day, says, "See, God provides. Nobody will starve so long as you put your confidence in God, in divine providence."

---

2 Testimony of Father Herman Buss in *Written Reports Concerning Fr. Solanus Casey*, OFM., *Cap.* June 4, 1984.

INTRODUCTION

Most of Solanus' listeners on that day of the Great Depression were too sunk in their own sadness or too hungry to draw out from his words any practical personal application. Most who wept did so not because they had been suddenly enlightened by a great truth that would remake their lives but because—amazingly, unexpectedly rescued—they were going to eat after all. Those without faith in supernatural realities may have chortled, "My lucky day," or the well-educated murmured, "A wonderful coincidence." Those with faith, most likely, would have been inclined to ascribe the "miracle" to the prayers of Solanus, obviously, from what had happened, a "holy person" with whom they had nothing in common.

What Solanus longed for others to grasp is the subject of this book: that if you're willing to open yourself to it, this kind of answer to prayer—demonstrated by saints of our time like Venerable[3] Solanus Casey—is available to everyone, including you.

This book, that is written for you with love from God, God's saints, and the author, braids encouraging, authenticated

---

3 Venerable, often shortened before a name to Ven. (similiar to shortening Saint to St. and Blessed to Bl.), is the title for those whose heroic virtue has been formally recognized and is an early state of the process toward official sainthood in the Catholic Church. Before heroic virtue is official, candidates are titled Servant of God.

incidents of how God met the financial/material needs of holy people from the so-called modern era (some canonized, some beatified, some on their way, and some just saintly folks whose holiness will never be recognized beyond a limited circle) with ways for *you* to position yourself to receive this kind of help. Called divine providence, it is the caring, providing, needs-fulfilling aspect of God. Each chapter covers a particular aspect of living in divine providence and suggestions, with examples from the saints, for reshaping your attitudes and actions to that end.

Need you become a saint? Let's put it this way: the surest way to receive a truckload of foodstuffs when you need it is to be holy. But I know a fairly large number of people who live by the guidelines in this book as best they can—Catholics, Protestants, Jews, and unchurched—who are not saints but whose lives demonstrate that these principles work. The book will report some of their prayer answers, too.

Living by these principles will lead you unavoidably toward becoming a better and better person. And since that's how one moves toward maximum human fulfillment and a joyous life after death, you could say that what you have here are guidelines for dealing not only with your material/financial needs but with your emotional and spiritual ones, too. In financial terms, you get "two for the price of one"!

CHAPTER *One*

In Life's Dance, Why Not Let God—Who Knows All the Steps—Lead?

NOBODY WOULD STARVE, SOLANUS ASSURED THE HUNGRY, SO long as they had confidence in God.

God wants to provide for everyone. Divine mercies fall like life-giving rain on both the just and the unjust. But if you put up an umbrella of self-sufficiency, anger, or disbelief, God respects your freedom to remain parched and dry.

Still, if you're tired of going it alone and want to live in God's providence, you can turn over your life to God's leadership. If you take a bunch of kids on a picnic, they expect you to provide everything. A life that is turned over to God—even though you'll need to do all the things common sense dictates to help yourself the way the kid has to get ready to go and feed himself—invites the same expectancy.

It's simple: just tell God you *will* to let him lead in life's dance (or captain your ship or guide you on your life journey—whatever metaphor you resonate to). If you turn around and find you're trying to run the show on your own again, don't be surprised. Laugh at yourself, if you can, and start over.

If the idea of God's leadership makes you have to pray, "I trust you. Help me trust you more," that's great, because it's truthful. Being truthful is absolutely essential in forming a real relationship with God, and it's true that trust has to grow in most people.

What if it's worse than that? What if your need for control is so great that giving your life to God is terrifying? If that's true for you, and you are in serious financial or other difficulties, try thinking of it as allowing a firefighter to lead you out of a building collapsing in flames. Or if things aren't that bad, picture yourself in any kind of a house being invited into a much finer, more spacious one. And keep pondering this: God does not want your surrender to enslave you. He wants your surrender to his loving leadership so he can free you from all those ideas, habits, and situations that imprison you—including your terror of losing control. He has no mold either: He loves variety and rejoices in your uniqueness, loving you with a completely unselfish desire for you to become all you can be. Your fulfilled life gives God glory and joy.

WHO NEEDS TO SURRENDER?

On the other hand, you may think, as a believer, you have no need to surrender. The life of Bl. John XXIII (d. 1963) can shed light on that. The impoverished, peasant sharecropper's son could never remember when he didn't want to be a priest. That his dream meshed with God's desire for his life was obvious when God provided the means through scholarships and gifts.

Still John, *like everyone*, eventually faced an important choice between "my way and thy way." In 1925, long before e-mail, cheap long distance, and other means existed to keep in close touch from afar, jealous people got the popular churchman exiled to remote non-Catholic Bulgaria. The transfer meant burying his gifts, loneliness, and isolation, hostility by the host people who feared and hated Catholics, and leaving behind his beloved family, hardest of all the two unmarried sisters who had lived with him. Named archbishop, which would mean nothing in Bulgaria, John took the motto "Obedience and Peace." He chose surrender to a plan he couldn't understand *and that made him suffer*, ignoring friends who urged repeatedly that he complain. Bishop John spent the next roughly twenty years in Bulgaria, Turkey, and Greece among wily monarchists and their determined Communist assassins, anti-religion republicans, and Fascist or Nazi invaders, and the guerilla movements opposing them. Religiously he worked with unfriendly Orthodox and wary Muslims, plus the imperiled Jews he helped rescue in World War II (he had already worked with Protestants and other non-Catholics as a military chaplain during World War I). Then he served nine years in secularized post–WWII Paris, among atheists, Socialists, and hardheads on both left and right. In a world suddenly shrinking due to new technologies, these experiences formed a man uniquely qualified for the papacy because of his wide understanding of other peoples, cultures, philosophies, and faiths. As for John's personal life, his experiences of God's care led him to dub himself "the son of providence." His wholehearted surrender also made him a saint, as well as one of the happiest, interiorly freest men in history.

Did you grow up with a dream? Often your dream is your dream for a good reason: it's God's desire for you too. Sometimes, on the other hand, God has a bigger, better dream that will bring you a richer life. Another saint exemplifies that. This is her story:

Imagine that you are little Francesca Cabrini, the youngest of a very big Italian family. You have your own unique dream. When you grow up, you are going to be a missionary to China. One day you are enjoying some sweets at a family gathering. To tease you, someone says, "Oh, Francesca, missionary sisters don't eat sweets." You swallow the mouthful with two feelings— a bit of sadness and a lot of determination. If sweets are going to stand between you and your dream, you don't want them. The teaser was only kidding. But you don't know that. You never take another sweet—not just that day, but ever.

Finally you grow up and after many setbacks—foremost that no missionary order will accept you because you are too delicate, too frail—you have become a sister. A priest, seeing that you would not give up your dream and no one would take you, directed you to found your own order. You have named it the Missionary Sisters of the Sacred Heart, because you are crazy about Jesus. You are going to take him to China so the Chinese can bask in his tender love too. Other young women have joined you, and you are ready to go.

And today, unbelievably, you have an audience with the pope himself! But what is this? Can your ears be working? No. No. No. The pope is saying, "Don't go to China. You are needed in New York and Chicago, Seattle and Los Angeles, in the Colorado mining camps and other places where your fellow Italians are dying without a word of comfort in their own tongue, where they are leaving orphans with no one to care for these children but well-meaning people who can't speak to them in their language and have no special love for—maybe even look down on—our Italian culture and religion. Take Jesus to America. Forget China."

If you cut your beautiful dream into little pieces and throw it away, because you see that what is wanted by the Lord is something other than what you have worked and dreamed toward your entire life, *that* is surrender at the heroic level.

Such a spiritual heroism led American naturalized citizen and patroness of immigrants Mother Francesca Cabrini to sanctity as a canonized saint and took thousands of people with her to holy lives and Heaven: North Americans, South and Central Americans, Europeans, and perhaps—in the divine economy, where things renounced for God can be offered up as prayer for others—a lot of Chinese too.

ACCEPTING A TWIST ON YOUR DREAM

Another form someone's call to surrender can take is accepting a twist on your dream. In the case of Father Solanus Casey, joy followed accepting a new, humiliating spin on being a priest:

Young Casey's love—after a teenage relationship didn't work out—slowly turned to God, not in bitter disappointment but in awe, wonder, and joy. Having learned to be comfortable with many kinds of people from such jobs as streetcar conductor and prison guard, he heard God's call to use his great ability to love others in the priesthood. Irish-American, he was permitted by God to have classes in Latin or German. Although he was smart enough, he had no flair for languages, and tackling complex subjects, such as canon law, dogma, and Scripture, in a foreign language proved extremely tough. In the end his unimpressive scholarly attainments led the Capuchins—who recognized his spiritual and interpersonal gifts—to offer ordination but only as a "simplex priest." This rare type of priesthood denoted that a man didn't "know enough" to preach on dogma or to hear confessions that sometimes involve complicated moral situations.

Hurt, maybe even indignant, Solanus swallowed his pride and surrendered to God's twist on the dream plan. Because of these limitations, he couldn't function fully as a priest, so he was given the lowly job of porter, the man who answers the monastery door. With this second surrender, Solanus was positioned to be God's instrument for thousands of physical, psycho-spiritual, and moral cures over his lifetime, as seekers of prayer, consolation, healing, financial assistance, food, or other help rang the bell. His life became fuller and fuller in joy as he gave himself away in service to humanity, living out God's plan for his priesthood. Many times he exulted, "All God's designs are wonderful for those who have faith."

Surrender—while it boils down to willingness to trust God's leadership—has many facets. Hopefully, you'll soon see more and more the wisdom of surrendering *everything* as much as you can. For example, here and in the next chapter are six additional, specific aspects of surrender with holy examples for each. The examples are plucked—take me literally here—from thousands of possibilities, since every saint has surrendered to God, either early or late. From them you can preview that by letting him lead, he will be able to do incredible things in your life, awesomely enlarging its possibilities and meeting your needs.

1. *Surrendering to God means giving your goodness to God.*

When you give your goodness to God, you give him your dreams, your talents, your special gifts, including those virtues that come easily to you or that you have acquired with hard work. There are countless gifts—yours might be engineering things or nurturing others, building houses or one of the arts, cooking, working with money or organizing things, or more subtle gifts such as the ability to see another's point of view that makes a mediator or the gift of prayer. Your virtues might include a cheery disposition, moral or physical courage, generosity, warm hospitality, or financial integrity.

One way of trying to let God lead when making decisions about developing and using your goodness is Ignatian discernment originating in the *Spiritual Exercises* of St. Ignatius Loyola. Ignatian discernment is an effort to recognize what's going on in one's soul based on feelings of consolation (peace, joy, contentment) and desolation (restlessness, anxiety, troubled unease). If considering a possible decision brings not momentary exuberance but ongoing feelings of peace and joy, while there is no absolute guarantee, it probably indicates God's design. Consulting trusted mature Christians who know you, such as your confessor or friends *who truly want what is best for you*, can be another way to find the path God has laid out for your maximum fulfillment. One way or another God will lead if that is your desire. Take two examples:

A man today titled Bl. Louis Martin dreamed of using his physical prowess, courage, and love of God as a monk in an Order that saved travelers in the high Alps. Sincere efforts in that direction just petered out. His continuing surrender to God led him step-by-step to become a successful businessman instead—not only a maker of fine watches with his own shop but also a successful investor. His desire to save others was fulfilled not only by those he physically saved from drowning, fire, or in wartime, but by his philanthropies, that included saving people who were down and out financially.

Around the same time, Zélie Guerin tried to take her gift of love for God into a convent but was told, "This isn't the life for you." Discerning this was true, she studied and learned a skill—in her case making the luxury good called Alençon lace—becoming a successful businesswoman with a number of employees. Her desires to serve God would be fulfilled not only in the way she treated her employees and those she did business with but in a holy marriage and family. Today, known as Bl. Zélie, the once would-be-nun discovered, "I was born to be a mother."

Although each had initially planned to live celibate lives in religious orders, Louis and Zélie met and married. Their marriage, rooted in God, was hugely successful, in their deep love for each other, that helped each other achieve spiritual greatness, and also as partners in business (eventually Louis closed his to take over the traveling portion of Zélie's), in charitable undertakings, and in parenthood. Had Louis and

Zélie insisted on entering monasteries, they would have never developed their great talents, not just for business, but for marital love and parenting. Themselves beatified saints, this couple became the parents of St. Thérèse of Lisieux and of Servant of God Léonie Martin.

2. *Surrendering to God means giving God all your interior ugliness whether small or large—even those failings and sins still hidden from you—by continually being open to acknowledge imperfections and humbly doing your best to improve.*

What this has to do with divine providence can be summed up as clearing space. Assume that your mental attic is crammed with unforgiveness, envy, resentment, and anger. All that baggage, perhaps accompanied by going over your "he/she done me wrong list" obsessively, can leave little or no room in your mind for reveling in God's goodness, his love for all (even those you hate), his mercy, and the wonderful way he meets your needs. Maybe under your rug is a trapdoor into sexual obsessions you turn to rather than deal with real relationships. That space could hold a lot of God's supply if you'd let him help you clean it out. Maybe your vault is so crammed with greed, there's no room for real riches. You get the picture.

This is not a book on inner healing. So let it suffice to say saints are people who, having surrendered to God, have with divine help cleared out all deliberate sin and the majority of their failings. Above all, they have wrestled into submission the pride- and anger-based trip-ups of good people: *righteous* indignation, *helpful* criticism, *justifiable* anger, *deserved* punishment, and other rationalized nastiness.

The space created is where the saint's heart, mind, and soul bask in God's presence and providence. So the more space you create—and this is a lifelong task—the more room you have for God's providential bounty of every kind.

Okay, so you're willing to accept that, if not a mean bone, there might be a mean sliver in your body. Surely God will not deny your needs by holding you responsible if you don't know you have various little meannesses inside? He won't, but it never hurts to open yourself to the need for repentance and change. To the degree you do that, you will receive from God, just for being open, as if you had already changed a great deal. (Scriptures actually *speak* about this in a parable of those who have done very little work getting paid like those who accomplished a lot because of the Master's generosity—look at Matthew 20:1–16, *The New American Bible*, Saint Joseph Edition.)

BEING READY TO CHANGE

How do you open yourself to being sorry for wrongs and to being ready to change? Cultivating honesty with God—who knows it all anyway and loves you way more than you do—is a key. In my case, I received the grace to pray, "God show me my faults." Well, the parade has never stopped. But God is as gentle as the best of mothers. He leaves a lot of distance, even years at times, between the revelations. Sometimes a realization arrives like Father Solanus' bakery man—just suddenly there. Other times insight comes through reading about the saints.

For instance, God once got through to me about gossip through reading about the parents of St. John Neumann (d.

1860), who are among the "hidden" saints of the world. Anyone who tried to gossip in the Neumann home quickly had the subject changed by Mrs. Neumann, and any guest who plowed on anyway was not invited back. I finally got it that *all* gossip was wrong, including the kind I excelled in, where you and a close friend talk about someone's faults under the guise of helping them through prayer.

Besides the flash insight or realization through reading, sometimes an area calling for change wells up in prayer. As the big areas get cleaned out, smaller ones come up and old resistances to change fade, seeing how each little bit of progress expands life.

As you ask God for help to live a life with more room for divine providence, remember: perfection is reserved for God alone. Even saints, to protect them from egotism, have imperfections to regret. Canadian Holy Cross Brother St. André Bessette (d. 1937), one of the Church's great instruments of God's healings, suffered fatigue-triggered crankiness, and oversensitivity that imagined censure where none was intended. He made frequent use of Confession, God's gift to those who sincerely want to change. Bl. Louis Martin's successful investments made him aware that, without watchfulness, he could become too caught up in the pleasure of making money. In Servant of God Dorothy Day's interviews with Harvard professor Robert Coles (published as *Dorothy Day: A Radical Devotion*), the founder of the Catholic Worker houses of hospitality is open about many spiritual struggles typical of holy people, among them struggling to serve, as well as to work with, others in a warm comradely, not condescending or indifferent, way, to do good year after year without self-righteousness or pride. In her personal diaries, edited by Robert Ellsberg as *The Duty of Delight*, Day records such self-criticisms as "I criticize [others while] I justify myself." The solution in her case, she feels—to avoid the implicit sense of superiority—is to consider everyone better than herself. (Obviously this would not be helpful to those with unhealthily low ego strength.)

Acknowledge but do not be lured into over-concentration on your negative traits. Insight into a fault that leads to self-condemnation is not of God. Recognition of faults that is rooted in God leads to real sorrow for them but concentration, with joy, on changing, not self-rejection. (It is God, after all, who asks us to set the bar at how we love our neighbor by how we love ourselves.) To make the process easier, keep your eyes more on the God of love (and if that isn't your concept of God, working on that is a good starting place) and less on yourself while you make more room for providence, through patiently and gently rooting out what slows down or halts the growth of your love of God and neighbor.

A LIFE-LONG PROCESS

Surrendering your ugly areas is always a lifelong process. When the middle of Zélie and Louis Martin's five daughters brought her outgrown dolls to the younger two, the young-est, Thérèse, put out her arms, crying, "I want them all." The future St. Thérèse of Lisieux gradually outgrew this childish greediness all the way to sanctity. She learned well that it's hard to receive God's bounty if one's hands are full of things snatched in greed, and that there is no need to be greedy if you live in divine providence. In fact, greed says, "I can't trust God to provide, so I'd better wade into life with both hands and grab my share—and yours too." Yet many of us who sincerely see ourselves as generous—and who *are* generous in many areas—have pockets of unacknowledged greed. These may be as simple as always snatching the biggest cookie, or the largest steak from the grill, stealing time at work for long personal calls, or taking office supplies for family use, or as insidious as wresting the last quarter percent of interest from someone who desperately needs a loan in hard times, or trying, perhaps at a garage sale or visiting an impoverished country to get some obviously poor person to sell you for less something you don't need and can easily afford. People who are basically good may do all these things without thought. But as you more and more desire to surrender, God will gently reveal yourself to you so you can blush and change.

Don't be surprised if God shows you the egotism mixed up with your virtues. For instance, you may *never* take the biggest cookie—and be very proud of that and feel quite superior to the cookie grabbers. Yes, egotism—usually unconsciously in the early stages of surrendering—is often found even in "doing good." I don't mean the egoism that is blatantly opportunistic, such as the man who told my relative that, now that he had his law degree, as part of his strategy for becoming important and wealthy, he was going to join the "best" community philanthropic group and the church of the town's movers and shakers. (Hopefully God laughed and snuck up on him inside the pew he entered only to feather his nest.) I mean the kind of hidden, subtle ego drives found in even saints-in-the-making. For instance, Ven. Solanus Casey's early desires to be complimented on his sermons or otherwise praised were only gradually overcome as he became aware of these yearnings and realized they were subtle forms of pride. And don't think you'll ever be egoless. The canonized St. Padre Pio said the ego *will* die—about ten minutes after you do. When you get glimpses of your egoism, do what you can to curb its driving your actions and enjoy a healthy rueful laugh at yourself when it does. Then look on the bright side: recognition of mixed motives brings the humility that is a tremendous claim on God's bounty.

In his seminary days, the future Pope John XXIII gained humility by discovering pride, ambition, and other ego elements mixed with his sincere desire to serve God and others, then struggled to give those weaknesses to God. In personal notes collected after his death as *Journal of a Soul*, he noted other realizations as he went through life and new surrenders, as well as gradual spiritual gains over the years in the areas of old conflicts. He acknowledged God's help by writing on the fiftieth anniversary of his ordination, "My merit: God's mercy."

You may find with John, as you work to make room for God and the freedom God brings, that some of the virtues you surrender to God at some point, oddly, need resurrender as weaknesses. For instance, John had a natural tendency to see the best in people and the virtue to never say to anyone else what he wouldn't want said to him. This goodness became a weakness when, as a bishop, he was charged with oversight of other priests. He struggled to do God's will in the matter, wasn't sure what that was, and finally concluded he'd have to lead by example not by dressing anyone down. A delightfully witty man, he blamed God "for sending Jesus to set me such a bad example."

LETTING GO OF UNFORGIVENESS AND HATRED

Probably the single biggest barrier to God's providence is deliberate unforgiveness and its partner, hatred, that is held onto and even justified. It's all right, it's virtuous, you may tell yourself—and many of us do the same—to hate terrorists, one political party (or the other), pro-choice adherents (or pro-life, depending on your view)—all those who are "bad." God has sad news if you see life that way: a person or group's political, religious, or other views differing from yours or mine does not make anyone "bad"—being misinformed, as another or an entire group may be (if it isn't you or I who are wrong!), never justifies hate. Even the terrorist cannot be hated—only his actions—because he is a child of God, who loves him. Maybe you can handle that, barely, but if it's an individual such as a family member, maybe an ex-spouse, or someone at your work who treated you badly, it's easy to feel justified in such hateful acts of unforgiveness as trying to get even and attempting to turn others, even children in the case of warring spouses, against your "enemy" as well. Forgiving seems something God would not expect *in this situation*. Well, bad news again: God may join you in hating the evil done to you—forgiving does not mean putting up with or condoning—but God wants you to forgive the doer of evil so you won't have to carry that terrible burden of hate. Or, as my aunt used to put it picturesquely, "Hate only rusts the vessel it's stored in."

Besides the harm it does to you physically, emotionally, and spiritually, hate ties you to the one you hate until you cut yourself free by forgiveness. If you have fallen into the devilish view that hate makes you powerful, be sure the fortress that hate builds keeps evil in and only bars the door to God, love, and good. It is not hate and unforgiveness but love and forgiveness that armor you against anything life can throw against you.

Let the following brief examples of forgiveness encourage you in the sometimes very hard but critical task of surrendering whatever grudges, resentments, hatreds, or other kinds of unforgiveness might wall you off from receiving all God wants to give you: When a man tried to assassinate St. John Bosco (d. 1888) because of Bosco's success in leading the young to Christ in the Catholic Church, Bosco built a home for his would-be assassin, whose bullet had missed by inches. He did this because "we should do good to our enemies."[4] And he did this work of charity secretly. (To demonstrate how Christians should live, Pope John Paul II, on the other hand, publicly visited *his* would-be assassin to forgive him.)

Oddly enough it may be easier to forgive a hired assassin than a member of one's own family. But Bosco forgave a half-brother

---

4 It is not doing someone good to let an individual murder you, of course. The powerfully built Bosco—who used to hammer a nail into the wall with his bare fists to delight the youth he served—any number of times fought off assassins who attacked him up close rather than by a gun fired through a window.

who forced him to become homeless very young to avoid this older kin's cruel abuse and to escape his own potential to sin by angry deeds in reaction. With hands not clenched in angry unforgiveness, but empty to receive, Bosco's life is full of amazing gifts of divine providence, some detailed in this book, to meet his and thousands of others' material needs.

The child later named Bakhita, or "lucky one" (d. 1947), a little girl of the Nubian Dagiu tribe in Darfur, the Sudan, used to look at the sun, moon, and stars and wonder, "Who is the master of these beautiful things?" She felt a great desire to see and honor him. One day the child was kidnapped, forced into chains, and after more cruel treatment, sold into slavery. Among her various masters were still more cruel people. One beat her daily. Another had the slave's breasts and belly decorated by razor, the wounds stuffed with salt so they couldn't close until the desired pattern of scars formed. Eventually she ended up owned by an Italian and was taken to Italy. There she discovered a new master called Jesus, who loved her. Eventually, Bakhita became Sister Josephine in the Canossian Sisters. She was notable for her gratitude to God for his gift of himself and for her great efforts at forgiveness of all who had used her so horribly. Once she said she would kneel before those who tortured her and kiss their hands because everything she had undergone had brought her to know God. As for the torturers' responsibility, she said they didn't act so much from malice as from habit, and she pitied them. Filled with this spirit of forgiveness and love, Bakhita was greatly loved in life and is a saint today.

Pope John XXIII was called a Communist or "Commie sympathizer" by good people filled with hate during the Cold

War. Even some in the Vatican schemed to paint him in ugly colors for the very deeds that saved the world from nuclear war during the Cuban Missile Crisis. John wrote an account for the historical record of one plot against him and on the margin noted, "I forgive and I put it from my mind."

Dutch Carmelite Bl. Titus Brandsma (d. 1942) in Dachau concentration camp forgave the nurse who, with others, was using him as a lab rat during one of the infamous Nazi medical experiments. He set in motion her eventual conversion, giving her his rosary and promising his prayers, before she murdered him with a lethal injection. She testified years later to this in the official inquiry that preceded Brandsma's beatification.

Brandsma was the exception. During WWII fear and hatred were normal reactions to Nazi cruelties. But when the older Dutch woman Betsie ten Boom (d. 1944) was taken apart by the Gestapo and brutalized to make her confess where Jews were hidden in the ten Boom home (he failed), this Dutch Reformed Church member's reaction was quite different. She told her sister Corrie, who rushed in to comfort Betsie when the Nazi left, "Oh, I feel so sorry for him." Betsie was taken to a concentration camp, where she died from the miserable conditions, but she would continue to feel only compassion for those whose spirits were clouded by brutality. To the end she dreamed of rehabilitating such persons—a dream that Corrie, who found forgiveness much harder, would actually bring to life after the war.

A good simple prayer to surrender unforgiveness is: "Lord, you know I have unforgiveness in my heart toward *N*. I don't want this. I *will* to forgive, and I ask you to bless *N*." Forgiveness is an act of the will. Feelings may take a long time, even years, to fall into line. *Don't let yourself think you haven't forgiven when old feelings well up.* When that happens, simply repeat your prayer and deliberately turn your mind away from those feelings toward higher thoughts—perhaps of one of these saints.

CHAPTER *Two*

Other Things It's Smart to Give to God

INVITING GOD TO LEAD IN YOUR LIFE BRINGS COUNTLESS BENEFITS. Here are four more areas it's smart to give to God.

1. Give God Your Image.

Here is another area in which one can become enormously freed, opening oneself to God's providence in a much more profound way. Most saints' lives testify that, whatever their good or bad reputation over the years after surrendering image to God, each eventually experiences in God a love that, whatever others think of them, makes life beautiful, worthwhile, and bounteous. Those who cling to some image of themselves never fully grasp or accept God's providence. To give God my image is a declaration of trust, that he truly knows what is good for me.

CONSIDER CHIARA LUBICH

Consider Chiara Lubich (d. 2008), foundress of the world-wide Focolare Movement. Chiara, age twenty-four, felt led to stay in her native Trent when her bombed-out family fled as the northern Italian city was pounded by Allied bombs in WWII. The young schoolteacher had definitively surrendered her life to God not long before. Now she was living with seven other young women drawn to her spirit. Racing to the bomb shelter, never without grabbing a Bible, these young Catholics under the pressure of imminent death heard via the Scriptures, *"Love one another as I have loved you,"* a radical call to live Christ's love even to the point of laying down their lives for each other. In their commitment to unity they discovered Jesus in their midst (Matthew 18:20). And amidst the destroying bombs, they decided to live for God, who alone cannot be destroyed.

Duccia Calderari, a woman who lived across the street, wrote a long account fifty-two years later of things she could never forget that began when she was rushing to the air-raid shelter. Rather than hustling to save themselves, a little group of young women were stopping to help children or the elderly. Two grabbed one stumbling old lady under the arms and ran her to safety. Duccia was amazed that people existed who put others ahead of themselves at such a moment. She writes: "I said to myself, *I have to meet those brave young women.*" She visited and became enchanted that each day the little group was reading the gospel and, without watering it down, trying to put it into practice. Duccia goes on:

> I recall the first time a person in need came to [their] . . . door. [They] . . . had read in the Gospel that morning, "In so far as you did this to one of the least of these brothers of mine, you did it to me" (Matthew 25:40). So they opened their pantry and gave this man everything they had . . . at the

risk of remaining without food themselves. This, however, never happened, because the more the number of people to be fed increased, the more . . . [they] received in food and clothing from friends and relatives. On one particular day they happened to give five eggs to a poor person, and that same evening they received a dozen.

Duccia and others continued taking note of this very different lifestyle, that didn't seem to be for show or an enthusiasm that would last only for a week or two. While Duccia did not join them, she found herself getting involved. An uncle gave her a pair of shoes. She says:

I decided to bring them right away to my friends . . . [With] the package under my arm . . . I saw Chiara coming out of the church . . . I said, "I have a pair of shoes for one of your poor." She . . . said, "I'm really very happy to see this."

Then Chiara shared with Duccia that a man with completely worn-out shoes had approached them that morning, and Chiara had promised him better ones without any idea how she would provide them. She and her companions had just finished praying for this need when there stood Duccia, the answer under her arm.

Nevertheless, what was the image of these young radical Catholics who were living divine providence so strikingly day after day? Duccia recalls that not all the townspeople were excited and inspired by the Focolare Movement,[5] as it came to

---

5 Foremost, for its Catholic members, this movement is about following Christ Jesus, who is "in our midst" even when he comes sometimes as Jesus abandoned and forsaken. And to follow him as he is followed by his Mother in her complete surrender to God; out of this comes love for all in

be called (*focolare* meaning "hearth" with implications of radiated warmth). There was perplexity and suspicion too. "[They] spoke of unity and they were taken for Communists. They spoke of the [G]ospel and they were suspected of Protestantism. They spoke of love and . . . were easily . . . misunderstood," Duccia explains.

Criticism and misunderstandings in no way caused Chiara to turn back, and the movement she found herself leading eventually caught fire and spread around the earth, 182 countries by her death in 2008. She herself was esteemed over much of her long life not just by Catholics, including her great admirer John Paul II, but by Buddhists, Protestants, Jews, Muslims, and Hindus. Individuals of all these beliefs "felt deeply understood by her" and saw her as a spiritual guide. All these groups—and non-religious ones, such as UNESCO (United Nations Educational, Scientific and Cultural Organization)—honored her focus on the spirituality of unity, fostering conflict resolution through interethnic and interfaith dialogue, respecting every person, and promoting philosophies and economies[6] of sharing rather than cutthroat competition.

God, thus the creation of unity with those around us, including all peoples and faiths, in turn fostering peace and human solidarity. Focolare's non-Christian members share the quest for loving unity as God's family or as a humanity committed to the good of all.

6 What Chiara termed the "Economy of Sharing" when she launched it in Brazil in 1991 (today the "Economy of Communion") is to run a business in spiritually sound ways, including sharing a portion of profits both to help those in need and to spread the "culture of giving." In 2010 there were 750 businesses around the world following the guidelines and thirty-three, Focolare-created, little cities whose inhabitants practice a lifestyle of human unity and economic solidarity as opposed to philosophies that promote competitive, even adversarial, attitudes.

Chiara's self-image was as a pen, brush, or sculptor's chisel—an instrument used by God to create something beyond her own or any human effort. She wrote that God's instruments (such as herself) were "small and weak" but formed by God through joy and suffering for the task entrusted to them. "At the appropriate time," she said, "one acquires a profound understanding of one's self and a certain insight into God, so that one can say with certainty, 'I am nothing; God is everything.'" (If you bristle at being "nothing," be assured this mystical truth in no way precludes having plenty of healthy self-esteem. Paradoxically, they go together.) Chiara can be held up as a poster figure (and future official saint) who shows that surrendering yourself, including your image, to God, most often results not only in your good works' making you loved but in becoming a light of God to your life circle or sometimes, as in her case, to the world.

CONSIDER DOROTHY DAY

Consider also Servant of God Dorothy Day (d. 1980), who grew up in a family, environment, and social circle where God was ignored or mocked. Hers was a lifestyle that encompassed all one might expect of a bright, idealistic, creative young woman from such a background: lovers, an abortion, impulsive marriage for the wrong reason and quick divorce, suicidal impulses (according to some), as well as radical politics. Her friends—the brilliant playwright Eugene O'Neil was one—tended to be troubled people who drank, sometimes did drugs, indulged in non-marital sex, and generally lived miserable, often tragic, personal lives in spite of, in some cases, considerable artistic achievement.

Yet Dorothy, having gone a long way down some wrong roads, found God waiting for her anyway; found him in a second pregnancy and the birth of her child by a man she loved but was not married to. Ultimately she had to choose between her long-time lover, a sort of common-law husband who was against the institution of marriage, Catholicism, and God. She chose God and a celibate life lived in the service of the poor as a laywoman and single mother. Ironically, Dorothy's old friends, as well as her child's father, far from applauding her sacrificial life, scornfully wrote her off as one of those Christian do-gooders. Some family members were disgusted with her too. Dorothy's own father, in a letter to a family friend, described Dorothy as "the nut of the family. When she came out of the university she was a Communist. Now she's a Catholic crusader . . . I wouldn't have her around me."

At first at least her image in the Catholic church was positive. Dorothy, serving the poor as a devout celibate who went to daily Mass and loved the saints, the Eucharist, and Jesus' mother, Mary, had admirers that included a Wall Street success turned New York priest from whom she sought advice on her marital situation. Years later, when James Francis McIntyre had become Cardinal of Los Angeles, he still gave her money when she came to Los Angeles and called on him, knowing her piety and the sacrificial way she helped the most unsavory down and out. But that was all he admired, so any money that passed from his hands to hers did so secretly. To McIntyre and the wealthy donors helping him sow Catholic parishes all over the open fields of Southern California—indeed to the American Church hierarchy in general and to most Catholics—Dorothy's image, from the 1936 Spanish Civil War, when she refused to support either side, to Vietnam, had become that of a dangerous anti-American. This was because she promoted pacifism. (The Church has room in it for saints who are warriors such as Servant of God Louis Gaston de Sonis, a French general, and for those who find war anti-Christian, such as St. Francis of Assisi and Dorothy Day.)

In her personal diary, *The Duty of Delight*,[7] Dorothy reveals a rare attitude toward her image. Repeatedly attacked, not just by the world and good Catholics but even by the Catholic Worker people she lived among on skid row, she wrote more than once of St. Francis' teaching on being rejected, not just by the world, but by one's own comrades, and echoed Francis by calling those experiences "perfect joy."

Yet with all the animosity, God saw her needs were met. Her diary entry for February 26, 1961, says, "It is a mystery to me how we keep going—these twenty-eight years, with nothing in the bank, and debts piled high. But we survive." Not only surviving, they were feeding and housing all the needy who turned up each day, whether there was room for them in a Catholic Worker house or someplace they had to rent, putting out a newspaper, and meeting dozens of other needs, including sometimes travel. Invited to Rome to fast for peace with other women during Vatican II, Dorothy was surprised, but not surprised, when immediately someone handed her $500 for the trip.

Both women gave their image to God. Chiara Lubich's brief period of questionable reputation didn't seem to bother her and was succeeded by long years of esteem and love. Dorothy Day,

---

7 Robert Ellsberg, editor (Marquette University Press, 2008).

rejected by just about everybody until the unpopular Vietnam War, rejoiced in being like Christ, scorned and despised.

CONSIDER CATHERINE DE HUECK DOHERTY

Servant of God Catherine de Hueck Doherty (d. 1985) is a third person who knew her ups and downs of reputation after surrender to God. Unlike the others, Catherine is an example of someone who, trying to do good and rejected undeservedly, suffered terribly but held on—barely some days—by faith.

As a near casualty of the Communist takeover in 1918 in her native Russia, the Baroness de Hueck (later Doherty) and her husband came to Canada as refugees. A beautiful and dynamic blonde with a title, Catherine went on the lecture circuit about her experiences to provide for her little boy and her husband, Boris, who was in poor shape after their Communist captivity. Before TV, interesting lecturers drew big crowds. Catherine was successful, highly paid, and experienced the good life, but she kept hearing God's call to something else. Eventually she gave up legitimate success to surrender to serving the poor, especially those whose lives, rich in discontent, attracted them to Communism's false face of brotherly love.

It is hard to believe, but having opened the doors of the first, thriving Friendship House (her missionary outreach movement), Catherine—probably a victim of jealousy, especially by a local pastor—found her reputation dragged through the mud. Rumor-mongers accused her of working for personal glory, thievery, or recruiting *for* Communism. Those churchmen who had previously befriended her shut her apostolate down. Although her heart was broken, Catherine did not say a word against them or make any effort to defend her work. She was penniless. She was going through an annulment from her husband, who had used the funds she earned to support his mistress and turn their son against his "gallivanting" mother. The boy had run away. Anyone who knew those things had more grist for the gossip mill.

During the 1936 Christmas season Catherine was tempted to suicide, so fierce was her pain. But she clung to the hem of God's garment. After experiencing a second similar blow in the United States trying to work for the poor and for racial justice in Harlem, she gradually became a venerated woman, fulfilled in a second marriage, seen as a great teacher and exemplar of contemplative prayer, and since her death, a candidate for official sainthood. But it must be said that surrender to God had not led directly to this reputation. Hers had been a long, rocky road. Years later she addressed God: "Twice I believed that it was time to bring forth fruit. But twice the storms of hatred, of scorn, froze the furrow . . . Then, when it seemed to me I died my thousandth death, . . .the sun came [out]. Beneath its warm rays I brought forth my seeds and laid them in your hands."

Settled in her last apostolate in Combermere, Ontario, where the practice and teaching of Russian traditions of contemplative prayer was coupled with outreach to the needy, Catherine and her fellow workers were so inundated with goods for the poor, they had to build new buildings to hold the bounty.

All three of these women's trials, including the marring of their public images during some periods, were the particular paths by which God led each to spiritual greatness.

Maybe as you contemplate your own surrender, you have neither the great grace (even most saints don't!) to want to be thought badly of, nor trust that you wouldn't be singled out for that fate—rather than be like the many saints beloved during their lifetime—if you "gave in" to God. Don't despair if you don't trust God. Instead, chew on this: God made you so that you and he can share a great love. God leaves you free because love that is coerced is not worth having. You can surrender to divine love or thwart your own deepest need. It will always be up to you.

2. *Give God Your Relationships.*

This is the smartest thing you will ever do. It does not mean losing anyone or any intimacy or benefit you treasure. In fact asking God's involvement in relationships of every kind is your surest guarantee they will be healthy and happy. Loving anyone in God—meaning to truly wish the person well—precludes all kinds of sick relationships. If you are in such a sick relationship, it will either completely change the relationship's basis to a new, happier one or get you out of it to your greater happiness. This is true even when it appears that someone must be lost: the relationship given up completely to avoid serious sin. When you are trying to live your relationships in God, even such "loss" is different and has a way of becoming gain—sometimes for both parties.

That happened to Dorothy Day when she had to flee to Mexico for a time to avoid the sexual-emotional temptation of her child's father, whom she loved but who would not marry her. As she said, she had to choose between this man and

God because the man was anti-God, anti-marriage, and anti-Catholic. The loss became, in her view, a lifetime of gain in the joy of living as a child of God, and her lifelong celibacy after this relationship is part of a whole heroically sacrificial life. Moreover the way she chose to deal with the father of her child the rest of their lives is part of the ascent to heroic charity that led Day to her place today as a candidate for official sainthood. It is also telling that, although he hated religion and the Catholic church, proclaiming himself an atheist, in his later years the man contributed to Dorothy's Catholic Worker ministry and wanted Communion when he was hospitalized.

Bl. Charles de Foucauld (d. 1916) wept when he left behind his sister, beloved cousin, and other relatives, to enter a Trappist monastery in his native France. But he discovered in his relationship with God intense compensations—probably best described as those experienced by someone leaving home for a far land to enter a rapturous marriage. The converted playboy aristocrat wrote, "Jesus is taking me by the hand, placing me in his peace, chasing away the sadness as soon as it tries to draw near."

Giving intimate friendships or spousal relationships to God opens the door to the joy and freedom found in loving someone properly—that is, the way your body-mind-soul is designed to love and be loved. As my author, philosophy professor, friend Ronda Chervin put it, "already in this life, if we are careful to purify our love of anything not of God, we can experience the joy of the union of persons which will be ours completely in eternity."

FRIENDSHIPS IN GOD

To see how friendships *in God* hold in check human tendencies to competition, envy, manipulation, overdependency, and other relationship-killers, investigate such recent holy friendships as Ronda's spiritual friendship based on what she calls "a mysterious grace-filled unity of spirit" with New York contemplative Charles Rich (d. 1998); John Paul II's friendship with Chiara Lubich and his "deep and intuitive" friendship "without a lot of words" with Teresa of Calcutta; or Bl. John XXIII's long friendship with Paul VI. Here the extraordinary friendship of two men of exceptional holiness and profound humility models what a relationship can be like, where each person values the other so much, his energies don't go at all into "tooting his own horn," so to speak, but into trying to give adequate expression to esteem, even veneration, for the other.

There are other benefits, as well. Fifty percent or more of American marriages dissolve in divorce. But marriages surrendered to God not only are provided for by divine providence, but just don't seem to end in divorce. Long-term God-centered marriages—where spouses are spiritual partners as well as marital—are joyous, not monuments to grim endurance.

What does a holy marriage look like? There are at least three examples relevant to our time. You can find one eavesdropping on the letters of St. Thérèse of Lisieux's parents Bl. Louis and Bl. Zélie Martin, each running a business while raising their five girls and Zélie fighting breast cancer. Check out, too, through one of their two children's memoir,[8] rough and ready Australian Frank Sheed (d. 1982) and his English "old Cathoic uppercrust," but equally feisty, wife, Maisie Ward (d. 1975). They were partners for God as pioneer lay evangelizing speakers, writers, and important Catholic New York City publishers. A third modern holy couple: hard-boiled, soft-centered celebrity reporter Eddie Doherty and God's woman in the slums Catherine de Hueck, each with other marriages behind them, she through a church annulment, he through two deaths. Eddie and Catherine's passion for God in no way precluded passion for each other. Emile Briére, a priest who worked with them intimately, writes:

> We witnessed their union over many years, and none of us can express their marriage in words. The depths of their love, their self-giving to the apostolate and their self-denial was a constant model and inspiration to all of us. Their love for God and the apostolate always came first, and their love for each other . . . second. [But] that they loved each other infinitely and incredibly we have all witnessed.

Surrendering children to God is also an act of wisdom. The surrendered child isn't idolized and perhaps emotionally and spiritually crippled—as in so many small families—by being more pet than person, materially inundated, and led to believe he can do no wrong. Nor is the child, in another perversion of God-intended parenting, seen as a possession meant to enhance the prestige of parents or live out their dreams—as described

---

8 Wilfrid Sheed, *Frank and Maisie: A Memoir with Parents* (Simon and Schuster, 1985).

in a *Fortune* magazine article[9] entitled "Assessing the Net Value of Children," with such laments as the trials and cost of getting a child into schools "that will not embarrass you in front of your pals." Whether written completely tongue-in-cheek, partially tongue-in-cheek, or seriously as it appears, I couldn't be sure. The article nevertheless reflects some real parent-child relationships.

A child abused in this way who became a saint is Bl. Pier Giorgio Frassati (d. 1925), who surrendered *himself* to God at a very young age. Pier Giorgio gave up the young woman he would have liked to marry and the profession he desired, due to the demands of self-centered parents completely blind to their son as anything other than a representative of their ideals, goals, social class, and lifestyle. Out of the relationship he had with God, Pier Giorgio found the power to love his spiritually impoverished parents in the same way he chose to give himself to the needs of the materially poor. Living with unfeigned cheerfulness, he became a role model of charity to his peers as he studied, climbed mountains, or skied with them—always quietly looking out for others and never hiding his love for God whatever others made of that. Only upon his death from polio at age twenty-four—a death made horrific by parental neglect and misunderstanding—when the church was packed with the poor and wretched Pier Giorgio had befriended, as well as the grieving friends and sports buddies of his own class, did his parents have a chance to glimpse the individual they loved as an extension of self but had never bothered to know.

People who surrender themselves and their children to God also avoid forcing a child to grow up too early. Bl. Laura Vicuna

---

9 September 14, 2009.

(d. 1904) had to live with and cope with sexual advances from her mother's boyfriend while her mother and her lover modeled not just immorality but a deeply abusive relationship. Laura, with the help of Salesian sisters, took Jesus' mother in place of one who couldn't protect her. Laura died at only twelve, not only offering her life for her beleaguered mother, but getting her mother's promise to disentangle her life from her abusive lover's. At the risk of her life the woman did, a mother taught courage by her child.

CONSIDER ZÉLIE AND LOUIS MARTIN

Contrast such "used" and abused children as Bl. Laura Vicuna and Bl. Pier Giorgio Frassati with children whose parents are *both* so surrendered they become saints: the case of Zélie and Louis Martin. The Martins demonstrate that, as sure as anything can be in this messy world, children with two holy parents will grow up loved, as if lent from God to be raised for heaven. That means neither being idolized and spoiled nor used, abused, or treated harshly. Among their five children the Martins had an ugly-duckling child, Léonie—who today is a candidate for official sainthood! So, if you are reading this and have a troubled child, be encouraged at what loving a child in God and your surrender to God's providence can do for one born with a difficult temperament or other problems. The five Martin daughters grew up well-behaved, loving God, and were each free to be herself, even if spiritual and emotional maturity took Léonie longer.

With one surrendered parent, it's harder to generalize. But take heart: plenty of good citizens and even saints have come from such backgrounds. Even if both parents are scallywrouds, a surrendered grandparent can be the catalyst for a whole, even holy, person.

3. *Give God Your Possessions.*

Don't panic: this does not mean you are called to give everything you own away and go live under some overpass! No, God needs the middle class, who are his hands in so many good works, and the rich whose generosity and means fund hospitals, universities, and other places where he is recognized, as well as those he calls to voluntary poverty. As for the involuntary poor, we can reflect that there wouldn't be many if ours were a thoroughly Judeo-Christian society living Leviticus 19:18, the Golden Rule. As for you, whatever financial abyss you dangle above at this moment, you won't be swelling their ranks if you grasp the principles of this book! And if the abyss threatening to swallow you is too much shopping, while you seek healing, maybe *if you can afford it* you can at least try to redirect your obsession toward buying for those who have real needs, whether relatives or the recipients of various clothing or food drives.

About surrendering possessions: it isn't what you have; it's whether it has you. Or to put it another way, it's what you do with it. Bl. John XXIII is a great example of not letting what you have, have you. At a certain point in the young priest's career, he was named to head a student hostel. Suddenly he had to furnish small personal living quarters for himself. John had an artistic bent and discovered he enjoyed "decorating" with the modest financial gift his dad gave him (unlike religious order priests, diocesan clergy take no vow of poverty). But he writes in his *Journal* that having set up his first home "in a suitable manner," God let him see more than ever the beauty of the spirit of poverty. He then prays that he will always "keep this feeling of detachment from anything that is mine."

In later years, rising to archbishop and then cardinal, Bl. John would enjoy improving the places he lived in—all owned by the Catholic church, not him. In Paris, where he served in the diplomatic corps, for instance, a benefactor helped him buy and repair tapestries to beautify the dining room. In his home village, he made gifts to enhance the parish church or to improve the rented quarters where his sisters lived and he vacationed, sometimes with churchmen in tow who would have been uncomfortable in peasant homes lacking amenities such as indoor plumbing. But appreciating beauty and what is suitable for a parish church, or for the official Paris residence of the diplomatic representative of the Church at large, never led John to set store by possessions. When his assignment in Paris ended, the tapestries remained. They had never been for him. So little money stuck as it passed through the hands of this "son of providence" that John easily achieved his wish to die poor like the follower of St. Francis of Assisi he was (as a Third Order Franciscan from his youth). Yet every one of his needs had always been provided for!

CONSIDER THE DREXEL FAMILY

There are people who live in well-decorated mansions who also never let their enjoyed possessions come between them and God. Consider the parents of St. Katharine Drexel (d. 1985), the American heiress. Katharine's father, Francis Drexel, and her mother,[10] Emma Bouvier Drexel, were one of the richest couples in America. They used their money to do immense good as philanthropists, while they enjoyed a town mansion (with a chapel), a country estate (where their daughters ran catechism classes for the workers' children), trips to Europe, and the best teachers for their children's private education. Reared to do good, the Drexel girls in turn lived exemplary lives, making praiseworthy use of enormous inherited incomes (to ensure that no one married any of his girls for money, Francis Drexel left all his wealth to charities, allowing his daughters to enjoy the interest on the immense sum during their lifetimes). Katharine, becoming a nun, dedicated herself and her riches to helping raise black and native Americans out of poverty through education. She became so detached from her resources—as the longest-lived she inherited from her sisters, each childless—that she never tried to break her father's will, that upon his last daughter's death left the fortune to charities named almost a century earlier, some of which no longer needed help. Katharine's order founded several schools—elementary, high, vocational, and

---

10 Katharine's biological mother died shortly after giving Katharine life; technically her "mother" was her stepmother.

even a university[11]—that relied heavily on this money. But if God wanted the schools to continue, she believed, God would provide for them. And he did.

Possessions also encompass opinions, ideas, even jokes. Did you ever bristle just a little bit when someone stole your best recipe and presented it to guests as their own? Ditto your best joke? To comment on this from a saint's perspective, I offer you one example from a number of types of non-material possessiveness that spiritual genius St. Thérèse of Lisieux (d. 1897) addresses in *The Story of a Soul*, the timelessly relevant autobiography she wrote under orders in her twenties. Thérèse writes:

> I used to believe I had no possessiveness about anything; but since I have really grasped what Jesus means, I see how far I am from being perfect . . . Our own thoughts, our own ardent ideas and feelings seem like a treasure which really belongs to us and which no one has a right to touch. For instance, if I tell a Sister about some enlightenment that came to me in prayer and if she later discloses it as if it were hers, I'm inclined to think she has stolen my property. Or if during recreation one whispers something amusing to her neighbor, and she repeats it aloud without saying where it came from, well, that strikes its author as a theft. She may say nothing of it at the time, although she would like to, but at the first opportunity she will delicately let it be known that her ideas have been stolen.

---

11 Xavier University of Louisiana in New Orleans, founded by the Order in 1925, is the only traditionally black Roman Catholic University in the United States.

With that lack of concern for image that marks true saints, Thérèse concludes her list of half a dozen forms of non-material possessiveness by saying, "I could not explain these pathetic human failings so well . . . if I had not suffered from them myself."

Of course, there are times when one has to claim one's ideas. Patents, copyrights, and such depend on staking one's claim. But would it really kill you if your spouse stole your joke or your friend your recipe? On the other hand, spouse and friend, wouldn't it be nice to tamp down your ego and give credit where credit is due? Those who do share rather than take the glory—remember Solanus asking everyone in the soup-kitchen line to pray instead of grandstanding by praying alone?—and who delight in others' possessions, whatever their form, as much as their own, are the ones among us who become loved. Solanus was called "the best-loved man in Detroit."

Another, sometimes deadly form of non-material possessiveness was touched on earlier with mention of parents treating children as possessions. Besides roadblocking an adult child's desire for a separate life, one with this blindness may monopolize a friend or be jealous if a spouse enjoys anyone else's company. As a widower St. Thérèse's father assumed he would enjoy his old age with one or more of his five daughters, married or single. As one by one they left him to become cloistered nuns, Louis Martin edified them as he does us today by swallowing his personal sadness and generously letting each child pursue her destiny. This renunciation led Louis deeper into God and helped make him a saint, as well. If possessiveness of people is a weakness of yours, pray for help to surrender, for healing of what's behind it, and consider apologizing to those you may have made suffer as you held them *too* close.

4. *Give God Your Inadequacies and Your Needs.*

Work at life, in the famous phrase, "as if it all depended on you," but keep reminding yourself that God will provide if, instead of insisting you can handle things alone, you hand him not just your goodness, dark areas, image, relationships, and possessions, but all the inadequacies you see in yourself and your needs, as well.

Inadequacies you see in yourself, whether they are objectively true or not—for instance, John XXIII all his life worried he was slacking in his work when he was actually conscientious—may make you feel God doesn't approve of or want you. That can block surrender. If you experience the temptation—and this *is* a temptation since it has no basis whatsoever in reality—to feel you are not personally loved tenderly by God, get a biography of Father Solanus Casey.[12] Just a few pages of how God helped good and bad Catholics, devout and nominal Protestants, practicing and non-practicing Jews, and people without religion when asked by one with trust in God's goodness (in this case Solanus) should clarify that no one is outside the parameters of God's love.

CONSIDER LÉONIE MARTIN

Certainly St. Thérèse of Lisieux knew that. She prayed for a killer rejecting God, who was to be executed, and rejoiced to see

---

12 See Sources on the Saints.

him grab and kiss the crucifix at the last moment. But one of her sisters did not understand the universality of God's love. Smack in the middle of an older pair and a younger pair, Léonie Martin was from infancy a frail, fretful child who, when not ill, had terrible allergies. Her sisters—all robust—were good-looking, bright, personable, gifted in various arts and spirituality. Léonie was less favored in every area. And it was she whom the Martins' housekeeper picked out for psychological and physical abuse that made the terrified child even more churlish, until the oldest daughter overheard something and Léonie was rescued.

But her mother died not long after from breast cancer, so the emotional healing foundered. Léonie decided to be a nun just as her four sisters would; but whereas the quartet were welcomed for their worth in Carmel, the ugly duckling whose behavior had gotten her expelled from school was sent packing by the Poor Clares and then the Visitation nuns—the latter twice.

Besides lacking physical strength to follow convent rules, Léonie simply could not overcome her feelings of inferiority and her anger. Although siblings, father, aunt, and uncle—her entire life circle—prayed and tried to give her enough love to heal her, the child of saints seemed destined to live and die pious but lonely, crabbed, and irascible. But God provided for her too.

Thérèse died vowing to fix things from heaven. Léonie was inspired to seek admittance once again at the Caen Visitation, where she had twice been tried and found wanting. Amazingly, new leadership there gave her the unheard-of third trial. This time she did more than succeed. Giving all credit to the prayers of her family and the spiritual guidance of her dead little sister, Léonie Martin became a new creation: sloughed off was the anger stemming from all her failures and knowledge of her inferiority measured against her siblings. Gone was the extra psychological damage from the housekeeper's abuse and her mother's untimely death. Today's candidate for beatification, who died at age seventy-eight in 1941, would have chuckled at the bishop of Caen's dubbing her "one of the hidden saints who sustain the world." But in truth she had become holy by her discovery of a truth she credited to Thérèse.

Here it is: just as the good mother is drawn to the child who needs her the most—the sick one or the one who wasn't asked to the prom, or the humiliated athlete whose failed catch "let the team down"—so God, who has the attributes of both ideal father and ideal mother, finds the human deficiencies, failures, and miseries of anyone who appeals for help, all the more claim on divine love. Truly the very reasons you are so sure God wouldn't help you, if you'll but ask, are your greatest surety of divine providence.

Beyond any inadequacies you may have that need healing, you are invited to bring to God all the other needs of your life as well, whatever they are. A special word though to those of you—mothers and other nurturers are particularly prone and so are successful men—who may be hampered in doing this because you are great at giving but terrible at receiving. If this is you, you probably picked up this book to position yourself to receive divine providence for others. As you read, you are likely thinking of your children's, spouse's, parents', friend's, or neighbor's needs. But the invitation is to *you* to bring God *your* personal needs. Far from selfish, *not to do this is to withhold from God the joy of meeting them*. Not that you can't pray for others: you note what Thérèse's prayers did for Léonie. Still, here's a place, maybe the only one, where "me first" is appropriate. Varying the old phrase, you need to willingly receive so you can continue to willingly give, and give with new power.

Happily, bringing needs to God does not demand a formal petition, and you can forget the stiff upper lip. St. Padre Pio counseled to go right ahead and complain to God about your difficulties and beg for relief. But Pio also advised that "at the apex of the will" you surrender to what God is doing or permitting. Father Solanus went so far as to urge, whatever the needs, thanks be given God *ahead of time*[13] as a vote of trust. And why not? The lives of the saints show amply that God can provide for those who follow him beyond their wildest expectations.

---

13 Thanking God ahead of time is not like some "prosperity" religion. That variant on Scripture teaches that you thank God and *claim* your prayer request. God will owe you and you will surely get what you have claimed. If you don't, you did something wrong, such as lacking faith when you made your claim. Our God is not a god on a string. Our God is a mighty God and owes us nothing. We thank God ahead of time because, in awe and worshipful gratitude, we know that, as Bl. Solanus repeatedly said, whatever providence designs is only for the good of those who love God. Paradoxically, this is a perfect fit with telling him our needs like little children. And, as Solanus laughed, like little children who expect only good from Daddy and Mommy, in a way our grateful expectancy "puts God on the spot."

CHAPTER *Three*

O Ye of Little Faith—in Other Words Most of Us

SURRENDERING TO GOD—EVEN WITH INSPIRING STORIES OF others who have—is easy only for the rare soul who receives an extraordinary grace, like miserable playboy-aristocrat-explorer turned happy, holy man Bl. Charles de Foucauld, who said: "Once I believed there was a God, I saw no other course than to serve him." Usually it's more *process* than a single act.

For example, you may surrender your life, but hold back "holy gossip," gossip in the guise of asking prayer for someone. You may give up all kinds of gossip the next year but still clutch tightly onto doing good things with a fairly strong motive of burnishing your good image. Three years later you may give up worrying over your image but refuse to surrender some other niggly little thing. Hilariously, one partially surrendered woman I knew was afraid she would be condemned to utilitarian white cotton underwear; no more colors, satin, or lace if she followed God wholeheartedly!

And the problem, person, or special need you hand over to God today, you may find yourself hugging to your heart again tomorrow. Or you may turn back from the new road for a time because it is, at first, uncomfortable or costs you—like the diminution of a cherished friendship you discover was based on malicious, fault-finding gossip.

Fortunately for you, if you have a problem giving up control in any of the aspects mentioned thus far—your money or sexuality, perhaps—you are only the latest in a long line of God's children with the same difficulty. And guess what: many saints fit in this category too.

This book limits its references to saints who are more recent for the sake of immediacy and the hope of absolute authenticity. Had we space we could go back to when (later St.) Thomas the Apostle one day cried enthusiastically of Jesus, "Lets go die with him" (I'm paraphrasing John 11:16), only to then fall apart and run like a rabbit not many days later from fear of doing just that. Thomas surrendered to God wherever that took him only after he received the grace of seeing Jesus in the resurrected flesh. From Thomas extends an unending line, people known only to God as well as the well known such as St. Augustine, who famously prayed, "Make me chaste but not yet"; or the nun later called St. Teresa of Avila who didn't want to give up those enjoyable gossip sessions in the parlor and used to shake her hourglass to shorten the boredom of prayer time; or the stylish young French physician, today Bl. Jacques Laval (d. 1864), indulging himself in fine horses, clothes, and furnishings, and dancing with beautiful women at parties, who told a sister scolding his worldliness, "I'm resisting God."

Consider even American heiress and eligible socialite Katharine Drexel, who, like her sisters, was deeply interested in the cause of those lowest on the American economic totem pole. She toured many Indian reservations and then went to Europe seeking personnel to run schools that she planned to finance to give disadvantaged youth a better life. But when the pope himself suggested she give *herself* with the money, her leap was at first more toward the door than for joy. In fact, as she wavered back and forth with an inner call to be a nun, instead of marrying like her equally philanthropic sisters, she wrote a memorable letter to her spiritual mentor listing all the reasons she should not surrender to that call. Among them: she didn't want to trade independence for community life, might be "maddened" by regular contact with people (read that "nuns") whose dispositions she'd hate, would find it "boring" doing the same things over and over, and might just "walk out." She didn't want to give up the luxuries money can buy either. She pointed out she was used to these—her family traveled in their private railway car like royalty, and had more money than a lot of monarchs. She also, like many, wealthy or not, didn't want someone telling her what to do and was sure she wouldn't do well under authority. What, she asked, if she was supposed to submit to leadership by someone "stupid and wanting in judgment"? She meant a mother superior, but many of us seriously doubt if God is smart enough to plan our lives—I'd better run things myself.

Eventually Katharine Drexel trained as a nun under a dread Mother Superior, survived, and became one herself, founding an order meant to improve the lives of Native Americans and African Americans. It has to be wondered whether, an invalid from heart disease for her last twenty years, Katharine noticed that, having finally surrendered her life, she received care from her spiritual daughters that, rich as she was, she would never have been able to buy. God will provide even for the rich!

CONSIDER MOTHER TERESA OF CALCUTTA

Mother Teresa of Calcutta was already a teaching sister, working as a missionary in India far from her mother, brother, and sister in her native Albania. In all eyes, including her own, she had surrendered completely to God. Only her confessor knew that she had even made a vow to refuse God nothing. She counted on God to be equally giving: with a building of school girls in her charge during a 1942–43 famine that took two million lives in India, on a day when the food ran out, she told the girls she was going out at 8 AM. By 4 PM, recalls one of the students, she was back with foodstuffs.[14]

In August 1946, on a day blood ran on the Calcutta streets in Hindu-Muslim violence, with three hundred girls and no food, she went out, passing horribly tortured dead. She herself testified that a lorry of soldiers stopped and told the nun she must get off the street. She explained she had three hundred students to feed and must take the risks. They drove her back to the school and unloaded big bags of rice. Again the one surrendered to God was provided for by God. It is not too much to say, as does Brian

---

14 See the testimony of a student who was there, in *Mother Theresa: Come Be My Light*, edited by Brian Kolodiejchuk (Doubleday, 2007), 36.

Kolodiejchuk, Mother Teresa's longtime associate and the priest postulator of her Cause for sainthood, that at this point she was "already a person of considerable holiness."

Then, through a number of mystical encounters, God began calling Teresa to give up her fulfilling teaching of girls from comfortable families—whose training in God's ways can bring society huge benefits—and her happy place in her well-established religious family. God wanted Teresa to go live among the poorest of the poor and found an order that an Indian girl could join without receiving far more than she gave; an order very poor, humble, and at the service of those at the very bottom of Indian life. Teresa had made that vow to refuse God nothing, *but* in a series of mystical encounters with Jesus (Teresa is one of those saints who hear his voice interiorly), what was being asked of her seemed too hard. As she put it herself, "To leave that which I love and expose myself to new labors and sufferings which will be great, to be the laughingstock of so many—especially religious—to cling [to] and choose deliberately the hard things of an Indian life—to [cling to and choose] loneliness and ignominy—uncertainty . . . these thoughts were a cause of much suffering."

To put it simply, vow or no, she didn't want to do any of this. She told Jesus with complete honesty that thoughts of living among—and worse *like*—Indian slum-dwellers "filled me with fear." She suggested that she should stay with the Loretto Sisters and become really holy by living the life of a hidden victim there. Jesus reminded her that she had, with the permission of her spiritual director, made that private vow not to refuse God anything. Interiorly she heard Jesus speak aloud some of her other fears: she'd lose her vocation, not persevere in such a radical life. He cajoled her: "When it was a question of your soul, I didn't think of myself . . . Now what about you? Will you refuse?" Over and over he repeated this question. He put into words for her other fears that she was unworthy and too weak to be, or bear the criticism of being, a European living among the poorest of the Indian poor. When she begged that he seek someone more worthy and generous of soul, he countered that he wanted her just because she was weak, incapable, sinful. . . .

He also "got to her" by saying that of course she didn't die for souls as he did, so she didn't care what happened to them. With such wily arguments, he finally won her consent.[15] The rest is history. What comfort that even someone who already loved God greatly had to struggle to let him lead in the dance!

Because of various misconceptions, some people recoil from surrender due to the belief God hates fun, that, in fact, he can be counted on to lay tremendous sufferings on those who give their lives to his keeping. As an antidote to such gloomy misunderstanding, consider four saints you've become familiar with. You probably agree that, if Solanus Casey, Chiara Lubich, and Zélie and Louis Martin had some human suffering, overall they still led joyous lives. Common sense teaches that everybody suffers. Those whose lives are surrendered find meaning and

---

15 Teresa's private writings that detail her struggles, including her letters to her bishop, were collected and published in 2007. See the previous note for publishing detail. The events are summarized by Kathryn Spink, as well, in her second book on Mother Teresa, *Mother Teresa: A Complete Authorized Biography* (HarperSanFrancisco, 1997), but Spink wrote during the saint's lifetime without access to the private papers.

growth, often joy in spite of trials, where others may find no meaning, consequent bitterness, and even despair.

I suggest those with the particular fear that God is grim and hates fun check out St. Philip Neri and other "Jubilation saints"[16] such as Bl. Titus Brandsma, individuals whose relationship with God evokes a joy so powerful it frequently becomes ecstatic. His Carmelite brethren frequently asked Titus to tone down his enthusiasm in choir, and overpowering joy so regularly hit Philip that, after he agreed to be ordained, he had to read his joke book before celebrating Mass so he wouldn't let his mind go to God and be swept up into ecstasy.

ATTRACTIVENESS: A WHOLESOME VIEW

Some folks fear that surrender means acceptance of a drab, dull life. One sees believers who won't dance at a wedding or attend the most innocent film, and wear ill-fitting, dowdy garb as if devotion to God requires unattractiveness. For a more wholesome view, look at photos of the very attractively turned out physician, wife, and mother St. Gianna Beretta Molla (d. 1962), or Chiara Lubich, whose Focolare emphasizes drawing others to God not just by smiles and joy but by human attractiveness. Chiara herself always looked lovely in modest clothing and well-coifed hair. Writer Franca Zambonini, who authored *Chiara Lubich: A Life for Unity*, saw Chiara's "perfectly groomed silver hair, her discreet elegance of dress" every bit

---

16 See *Crisis* Magazine, March 1998, Vol. 16, 28–31, "Saints Who Laugh," by Patricia Treece.

as much as her "ready smile" and "unfailingly pleasant manner" as reflections of her spirituality. Catherine de Hueck Doherty, although she worked in slums, was every inch a woman who liked an attractive dress even if it came out of a giveaway bag, and put on her lipstick until told to give it up by her spiritual director. She presented outer and inner beauty that grabbed the eye and heart of a worldly man who became her second husband, a model Christian, and eventually a priest in the (marriage-permitted) Melkite rite.[17]

Another difficulty may come from an overinflated view of what trusting God means—as if you must toss your humanity out the window. Mother Angelica of Eternal Word Television Network (EWTN) is a down-to-earth, feisty Italian-American who once told interviewer John T. Catoir, "Faith to me is one foot in the ground and one foot in the air with a queasy feeling in your stomach . . . It's uncertain sometimes. It's negative. It's anxious. It's frustrating, and it gets you angry. You know, I get so angry at the world, at my crew, at my sisters, even at the Lord, but for me that's all part of faith."[18] Mother's impulsive

---

17 After some years of marriage, with his ordination at age seventy-nine, he and Catherine chose to sleep apart and practice celibacy. Don't take from that decision, right for them, that God is against sex even for the elderly; the beatified Martins, confused about sex when married, thought they should be celibate to please God; a priest talked them out of that, as nine children evidence; theirs was a wonderful, full marital relationship. Dorothy Day chose celibacy when the man she loved refused to marry her but was certain God wanted people to enjoy marital sex. Charles de Foucauld, who flaunted his mistresses, later found "chastity became for me a sweetness and a need of my heart." Every spiritual journey is different, even in sexuality.

18 Father John T. Catoir, JCD, *Encounters with Holiness* (St. Paul's, 2007), 159–71.

behavior whenever she thought God was not getting his due got her into hot water with important churchmen, including American cardinals, during one period. Yet her overall devotion to promoting the gospel led the pope himself in 2009 to award the *Pro Ecclesia et Pontifice* (for service to Church and Pontiff) Cross[19] to the EWTN foundress in spite of her temperament, that was both her cross and allowed her to achieve great things for God. Your imperfections and humanity will not keep you from service to God either.

Your difficulty in surrendering to God's leadership may be uniquely your own. Just know that God will accept you as you are, spiritual warts, sins, and all. But if your attraction to some particular thing you know in your heart or conscience is bad for you but you don't want to give up—workplace practices, relationships, uses of your sexuality, escapes from reality that risk addiction, to name a few—is making you keep the door closed to God, *try not to kid yourself it's something else.* In the view of Bl. Charles de Foucauld, for instance, he had many intellectual problems preventing belief. They vanished when he confessed his moral sins, indicating his choice to sin, not intellectual issues, had been the real problem all along. If you are ensnared and can pray sincerely for help, help will come. Others' prayers can be a powerful help as well.

Sacramental confession is also powerful. An atheist doctor suffered from epilepsy. As a man of science, the doctor kept notes on the physical healings God provided through St. John Bosco and then sought the priest out for his own cure. "Very well. Kneel down and confess your sins," Bosco said. "That's

---

19 The highest papal honor that can be given religious or lay people.

what I can't do. I have no faith," the doctor replied honestly. Bosco paused a minute, then the curly-haired saint smiled his obstacle-melting smile. "But you have *some* faith, or you would not have come." Somehow the doctor found himself on his knees, rising from confession a man simply remade. As for the epilepsy, it was gone.

That there *is* some link between God's providence and the willingness to give up acts that defy the Ten Commandments is witnessed by events in the lives of many saints, including St. Jean Marie Vianney (the Curé d'Ars; d. 1859), parish priest *par excellence,* and humble Holy Cross Brother St. André Bessette (d. 1937). The Curé told a young woman she'd receive the physical healing she asked God to provide gradually as she changed the way she spoke to her mother. She took his advice and was healed. Holy Cross healer St. André sorrowed over a man seeking physical healing but unwilling to surrender an adulterous relationship. The man went away unhealed. His obstinacy apparently blocked God's working through St. André. More recently, Father Aloysius Ellacuria (d. 1981) was God's instrument of healing twice for a seriously ill man who promised to change his life if healed, each time didn't, and got ill again. Eventually the saintly priest felt he couldn't continue to ask God to physically heal a person who simply wouldn't take God seriously.

Whatever the obstacle that bars your door to God and his providence, the following will probably help. *If you can't surrender all the way, surrender anything you can to get even an arm, so to speak, under the sheltering roof of divine providence.* Maybe give up bad-mouthing someone whose faults you love to advertise. If you can, use your will to at least tell God you desire to surrender more. If you can't honestly say that, perhaps you can say you wish you could. Honesty about where you are and any prayers for help to move forward are very pleasing to divine providence, it appears, from the answers received by many who have traveled this road. Look at that long-ago man who told Jesus Christ, "Lord, I do believe; help thou my unbelief" (Mark 9:24). God provided for him the desire of his heart.

CONSIDER CATHERINE AGAIN

If you not only can't believe but maybe don't even want to—this book having fallen in your lap, so to speak, through no desire of your own—consider an event involving a person who perhaps disliked "all this God stuff" even more than you do and Catherine de Hueck. While she still lacked absolutely rocklike faith that God would answer her prayer by providing what was needed, as it was needed, Catherine had the following experience described in a chapter she called "A Drama of Faith" in her book, *Not Without Parables*.[20] It was corroborated by one of those who worked with her, who described the incident to Eddie Doherty after his marriage to Catherine. Summing up the long detailed account:

It was a severe winter early in the great economic depression of the 1930s. Friendship House in Quebec, not yet closed down by its Catholic sponsors, was down to its last scuttle of coal.

Without coal there would be no heat and—the kitchen range also used coal—no hot food. Needed was about half a

20 *Not Without Parables: Stories of Yesterday, Today, and Eternity* (Madonna House Publications, 1989), 51–56.

ton, and there was no money. What, asked the cook in front of the seventy sheltered there, did Catherine propose to do about it?

Catherine knew there was no money to meet the need. She writes: "Prayer was the only answer I knew of, a prayer of trust in God and in his divine providence." She told the cook and the roomful, "We would have to ask God for the coal, ask him simply, humbly, in utter faith, adding a little postscript that 'because of this emergency and the falling temperature, we need the coal *today, before four o'clock in the afternoon.'* " She set that deadline because the coal they had left would be used up by then. She got on her knees, the non-Catholic cook got on his knees, a lot of the guests got on their knees.

"A deep, mocking voice," as Catherine described it, broke in. Scornfully, he spouted the Communist line, insisting this turning to God was "foolishness" and all religion only "the opium of the people." Catherine ignored the tirade, that continued as she and many prayed the *Our Father*, the *Hail Mary*, the *Glory Be*, and she spontaneously reminded the Holy Spirit, whom she called "the Father of the Poor," and Jesus' mother, Mary (who successfully took another group's need to her son at Cana), about the problem and the deadline.

After that they all got up and everyone went back to what they were doing.

God didn't exist, the heckler declared. He'd stay to ensure Catherine did not sneak out to phone for help and be there to laugh at her at 4 PM.

He went on and on with his harangue as the afternoon slipped away. At one point Catherine asked him what he would do if the coal arrived. He said he would try to look into religion and God with as open a mind as he could.

Catherine had seen the needs of this ministry met time and again in ways that could only be considered miraculous. But now, as the ticking of a clock went on and on, she began to worry. She describes her feelings: "Had I been too presumptuous? Had I overstepped . . . in my inner certainty that God and our Lady would hear our simple prayer and answer it before four o'clock? Could one do that, set a time limit on God's providence?"

Aware that, beyond the coal, a man's soul was involved, Catherine kept praying. The clock ticked on. Two o'clock, three o'clock, three thirty, a quarter to four, ten to four. The man was laughing. Catherine later remembered, "My heart felt heavy, and my soul darkened for a moment. Of course I had been presumptuous." At five to four, she felt like weeping as the jubilant harasser babbled on, "straightening out the thinking" of seventy morose men even as the last bits of coal were being consumed and cold opened its mouth to bite through scrawny flesh into bone.

It was one minute to four when the door suddenly swung open. Catherine later wrote, "A dirty-faced man with a dirtier paper in his hand stamped off the snow." He wanted to know if this was Friendship House. He had orders to deliver a ton of coal there.

The clock clanged four.

Catherine's long account ends without saying whether she ever found out whom God inspired to send the coal. That it arrived exactly at four was enough for her to know that it came from divine providence, whoever was God's instrument.

On the surface this story is about a woman who had a lot of faith but wondered if she had offended God by saying the coal was needed by four o'clock. Would God show her not to make such demands by either not sending the coal or by sending it hours later? Catherine hadn't yet become childlike enough. After all, when the second grader tells a good father he has to have the field-trip money by tomorrow morning and gives the precise amount, Dad does not take offense that a certain thing is needed at a certain time. God doesn't either. In fact, God, it appears from the lives of the saints, loves that complete trust children give good parents. In this event, God showed Catherine that pinpointing the need is okay when it's legitimate and the motive pure: Catherine wasn't showing off; she had seventy men in danger of cold and hunger. She had surrendered all she had to give. God took it from there and did provide—not half a ton but a whole ton, twice the amount asked.

Actually the story is less about this saint in the making and more for those of you—that's maybe 99 percent of us some days—who can't surrender or even believe in God's reality, power, and love—finding the whole notion of divine providence too much to take. "You're foolish: there is no God. No divine being cares," the mocker scoffed. After the coal had arrived, just at the moment of need, Catherine heard him mutter, "Nazarene, you win again."

The man who could not believe in God's reality, let alone in divine providence, became a priest. Perhaps through Catherine's heartfelt, anguished prayers or just out of the lavishness of divine mercy, God provided for him too.

CHAPTER Four

Grow Your Faith

A PARABLE

THERE ONCE WAS A FATHER KING WHO HAD UNTOLD RICHES he wanted to share with his grown children. He created a beautiful place filled with delights and sent each an invitation to arrive there anytime, day or night: the gate would never be locked. All within was for their joy.

Now, among the King's servants was one who was false. Finally the King had to dismiss him for open, armed rebellion. The fallen servant had wanted to replace the King and control all the riches. In his ugliness of soul, he felt no remorse for playing the good King false. Now his heart was too hardened by hate to enter the beautiful place and partake of the King's lavish generosity. Since they could not be his, the evil one wanted to be sure no one else entered the gate to enjoy the delights the King had prepared for them.

This enemy of the King also sent messages to each. He whispered almost imperceptibly into their ears. He put up signs and wrote articles, books, made films, all filled with the message: don't accept the King's invitation. It's a trap. If you enter the gate, you'll be enslaved and either forced into drab drudgery—say good-bye to fun—or you'll be tortured night and day with all kinds of pains and sufferings. Either way your life will be ruined.

Many believed the wicked messages. They stayed outside the King's place, and one by one they *were* drawn into lives of drab drudgery, in a place where the King's invitation was almost forgotten among those much louder and more alluring voices. Blinded by their growing inner darkness, the King's children became easy prey for tempters who promised delights that at first enchanted and then lost their color and flavor. Some people actually became enslaved to things that led to the pain and suffering they had tried to avoid by heeding the call to reject the King's invitation.

Others, however fearfully and timidly, opened the ever-unlocked gate and stepped inside. "I'm afraid. They say he piles on the suffering. But the Father King just draws me. For me, I guess it's better to suffer and surrender to this longing to find him than to play it safe outside," sighed one. This person had slipped in before daylight so as not to be seen and scorned by the multitude.

As the dawn came up, the timid one's eyes grew large.

"Oh my!"

"I didn't know!"

"Oh, Father!"

"All this waiting for *me!*"

"Oh, what a fool I was to listen to any voice but yours!"

And another soul ran to enjoy the Father King's company and all the good things prepared for those who accept the invitation to share in the riches of divine providence.

The enemy of our soul is always trying to minimize and to hide the blessings by which we are continually surrounded.

— Father Solanus Casey

No one stays the same spiritually. Faith grows or it wanes. The good news is that whatever degree of faith you have, you can grow it the way people who end up saints grew theirs. Day by day, moment by moment you can learn to opt for trust, hope, and joy and move away from cynicism, bitterness, or self-pity. Making serious efforts in this direction will go a huge way toward positioning you to have your needs met by divine providence. Here are some practical suggestions:

1. *Talk about your experiences of divine providence and those you learn of—maybe even regularly exchange stories with someone growing their faith too—in order to put you on the lookout for the instances all around you.*

Here's a simple example. You drive to an appointment with only five minutes to spare. The parking lot is jammed. You say with all the faith you can muster, "Lord, I need a parking space." Someone suddenly backs out and in you go. This is divine providence. Share it. Look for someone who will listen and then say, "Now let me tell you what God did for *me* today!" rather than speak about it to the jaded soul who, instead of rejoicing with you in this evidence of God's care, will pooh-pooh what happened as "just coincidence" or make fun of your simplicity. (Later, when your faith is strong, you'll be able, maybe even eager, to share with such people without hurting yourself.)

As to the sudden availability of the parking space, I first learned about God's providence in such small details of life from studying Basque-born Claretian priest Father Aloysius Ellacuria through interviews with those, from engineers to cloistered nuns, who knew him. About Father Aloysius, whose Cause is in the preliminary stages, I'll stick my neck out and say simply, "He'll be canonized one day, and if you can find any of the books by those close to him, you'll know why."

Stationed the last years of his life in downtown Los Angeles, Father Aloysius did not drive but was in great demand, due to his holiness and charisms, such as the gift of healing, to visit people all over the vast Southern California basin. Volunteers drove him, sometimes having to set out in the worst rush-hour traffic. But if you went with Father Aloysius, besides being certain you'd spend most of the trip in prayer saying the Rosary, you could also be certain the way would open like a hot knife through butter. You would travel the most awful freeway as if it were midnight instead of perhaps 5 PM.

Father Charles Carpenter has written about this in his book on the priest he considers his spiritual father.[21] Carpenter spent four years working for the Claretian priest before beginning studies for the priesthood. Then a young Peace Corps returnee, one day he was driving Father Aloysius to the Los Angeles Cathedral to join other priests in concelebrating Mass with the city's cardinal. The city's freeway traffic was so bad, it seemed impossible to arrive on time. Father Aloysius invoked God's great archangel Michael and blessed the traffic. At once it began

21 *The Life of Father Aloysius* (Missionaries of Fatima, P.O. Box 10006, Torrance, CA 9050).

to move briskly along, permitting—admittedly with no time to spare—an on-time arrival.

We can also be encouraged by the woman I know well who has not lacked parking spaces for decades with her simple prayer, "Lord, we need a parking place," said, she confides, with faith and awe at God's loving providence for her small need.

2. *Immerse yourself in authenticated instances of God's divine providence.*

You might even want to keep a notebook of such instances. If you develop the attitude that looks for such things, true instances of divine providence may be found, not only in religious magazines with reputations for truthfulness such as *Word Among Us*, *Catholic Digest*, or *Guideposts*, but even in the secular press. I think of stories, for instance—each in at least one major U.S. newspaper—about the unusual safe landing of a plane on the Hudson River in New York City in January 2009. Or about the Los Angeles Catholic Worker (a fruit of Dorothy Day's life), with only $10,000 in hand, having only thirty days in 1978 to raise an additional $55,000 or lose their building in L.A.'s downtown district of misery. It was a huge sum for this little charity. Mother Teresa providentially visited them at that time and said, "Don't worry, you are doing a good work here, and God will help you." Her advice: "Write a letter telling your need to St. Joseph and hang it around the neck of his statue." Very polite to their venerable visitor, when she left, Jeff and Catherine Deitrich and their co-workers had a hearty laugh. Tieing notes to saints' statues was definitely not their style. But two of the staff actually wrote a letter and trotted it over to St.

Joseph's Church, where they left it hung around the neck of the saint's statue. The needed sum arrived almost immediately.[22] This story made it into the *L.A. Times*, as did an article on the inexplicable energy ascribed by the article writer to the prayer life of the aging John Paul II making visit after visit in Africa in sizzling weather that laid low everybody with him, including the press corps in 1982.

Search out books (such as this one) that will encourage your faith in God's providence. To motivate you, here are three amazing instances having to do with a saint from authenticated materials. That is, each is by an authoritative writer on that saint—a witness who was there, or offers a verified[23] first-person testimony.

THE EXAMPLE OF MOTHER CABRINI

Picture Mother Cabrini in a strange land where she knew no one but the only One you have to know to go into a city penniless and soon put up a hospital (she did that in New York,

---

22 This incident was verified with Catherine Deitrich of the Catholic Worker house. She and husband Jeff were the house leaders when it took place, as they remain.

23 When permitted to work in the archives at Lisieux, I was greatly reassured about the miracles through Thérèse reported by scads of handwritten letters because the Carmelites and others had wisely asked that the writer have someone such as their parish priest write an accompanying attestation of the letter writer's honesty and mental stability! Or, as someone once complained, "Hey, a lot of people with mental problems think God is doing special things for them too."

Chicago, and Seattle), an orphanage (in Colorado, New York, and Los Angeles, to mention three), dozens of schools in various countries throughout the Americas and Europe, and other institutions to bring God's loving care to others. She kept them running for decades too. At night she has to sleep in a room alone because the glory of God tends to light up the space and wake companions, which is of course offensive to the humility of one who no longer thinks of herself at all, so madly in love is she with Jesus. Mother Saverio De Maria, assistant, secretary, and constant companion on Mother Cabrini's travels for these undertakings, wrote a life of the saint.[24] Mother Saverio recalls that many people offered Mother Cabrini financial help, but she accepted from very few. Among the reasons she did so is this utterly delightful one: "Her trust in divine providence was so limitless that it seemed unfair [to her] to seek other support."

Now picture a day like many when this consummate businesswoman (as people who had dealings with her described Mother Cabrini) is told a tradesman is at the door, seeking payment of his bill. The saint hands to another of the sisters the key to the desk money drawer.

"Empty!" she reports back to Cabrini.

Mother De Maria writes: "Mother [Cabrini] concentrated a moment, then, with serene tranquility said, 'You did not look well; look again.' Sister opened the same drawer and found a small package of brand-new bank bills—the *exact amount* required to pay the bill. Our dear Mother, while recounting this fact (just to her daughters) many years later with eyes full of gratitude

---

24 Mother Saverio De Maria, *Mother Francis Xavier Cabrini*, trans. Rose Basile Green (Missionary Sisters of the Sacred Heart, 1984).

and love, used to add: 'How many of these occurrences I could tell! Truly the Lord overwhelmed us with his benefits.'"

Another time a sister needed to pay off a bill, but there was no money. "Why don't you put your hand in your pocket?" Mother suggested. Without thought, the sister did so. There, as before, was the precise amount needed.

Mother Cabrini died early in the twentieth century. Let's jump forward to another Italian foundress, Sister Elena Aiello, who died in 1961. Her story is told by another authoritative source, Father Francesco Spadafora, who knew her well and collected others' first-person testimonies as well. The order founded by Aiello in her native Calabria has as a primary apostolate the care of young girls who have lost their parents one way or another. To provide the food and other necessities for these youngsters, Father Spadafora writes that "Divine providence . . . never failed to take care of what was needed even by means of extraordinary interventions." Among those Father Spadafora cites is an "extraordinary intervention" from September 11, 1935. At the orphanage where Aiello was living, there was no food for the next meal. Just as one of her sisters asked Sister Elena for some money, a priest arrived wanting to say Mass. The foundress, who had no money, told the sister to go to Mass and after it God would provide. At the elevation of the Eucharistic Host "a strong fragrance" spread through the chapel, a sign, as far as the Sisters and their orphans were concerned, that God was acting. Sister Elena, using her prayer book at that moment, suddenly noticed fifty lire between two prayer cards. Father Spadafora writes, "She was positive that nothing of the kind had previously been in her prayer book."

She had the previous evening read the same prayer from that same page. But she recognized there was always the chance some charitable person had managed to slip money into her prayer book as an anonymous good deed. With the childlike trust that characterizes people such as Cabrini and Aiello, Sister Elena was heard by a number of people asking God to show her if it had been divine providence acting directly rather than through a human benefactor by letting another fifty-lire banknote appear in the same place. Mass ending, she left the prayer book in its usual place. Over the next hours some of the Sisters and older orphans kept checking the book to see if more money had materialized. None had.

Evening came bringing community prayers. Suddenly all perceived the same fragrance as before.[25] Father reports, "Sister Elena got very excited. She didn't dare open her prayer book, but passed it to Sister Teresa to do so. Sister obeyed and there were the additional fifty lire between the two prayer cards."[26]

---

25 See my book *The Sanctified Body* on the form of this spiritual perfume connected with saints, known as "the odor of sanctity."

26 Of course, there is some possibility that a benefactor got to the prayer book, but getting into the chapel without being noticed by some Sister or child, especially that day, would have been difficult. And who among them would have dared help deceive in such a serious question as whether divine providence was acting directly? Strongest in favor of the lire coming from God without intermediary is the supernatural odor each time the phenomenon took place.

THE CHEERFUL HOLY BEGGARS

There are many similar stories of Mother Teresa of Calcutta. For these, my authoritative source is Kathryn Spink, a longtime associate of Mother and her co-workers, lay and religious.

In the beginning years, Mother Teresa and her first Sisters went cheerfully begging around Calcutta "for their poorest of the poor" but never asked anything for their own needs. God provided those. As the order became known the world over, "Increasingly," Spink testifies, "Mother Teresa stressed that fundraising for her work was contrary to her wishes, and she declined the offers of regular income that were beginning to arise," her attitude similar to Cabrini's: if God wanted a work, he, Master of the universe, would provide without a fundraising arm to the Missionaries. Thus, when her Sisters came to Harlem, New York, Mother Teresa turned down the offer of a monthly subsidy from New York's Cardinal Cooke, teasing him: "Do you think, Your Eminence, God is going to become bankrupt in New York?"

Mother Teresa told her Sisters and other co-workers, says Spink, that their work must remain one of love, not become a business in any way. "I want you," she urged, "to have that complete confidence that God won't let us down. Take him at his word and seek first the kingdom of heaven, and all else will be added on." So Teresa and her family-in-God strove to seek God and let God provide.

God did: In Calcutta one day there was no food and seven thousand mouths to fill. Just then the government closed all the schools for some days and sent the food provided for schoolchildren to the missionaries. Another time in England,

Mother Teresa proposed to open a house in Southall, but the one she thought suitable cost £9,000. The owner, out of love, came down to £6,000. Mother, unable by Indian law to bring out any money, as she went about a preplanned tour in England, mentioned the possibility of opening this novitiate. She made no appeal for funds, but at the end of her tour, her old knitting bag, says Spink, was stuffed with donations that added up to £5,995. For Mother this was God's "go ahead" that he wanted the foundation in Southall.

With stories like these in your notebook, even if just quick jottings, how could your faith in God's provision not grow?

Maybe you absorb better by hearing or seeing rather than reading. You can find radio shows, CDs or digital audio files, video and films, and other media that will build your faith as you drive to work, jog around the block, walk the dog, or relax at home. Check contemporary films reviewed in Catholic or your church's newspapers. You can go online to seller sites like VisionVideo.com, peruse non-selling sites such as Insidecatholic.com for *The Fifty Best Catholic Movies of All Time* by William Park (missing, naturally, all those since he did his list in 1999), find the Vatican's list of one hundred best films, or browse uplifting sites hosted by many other groups. One film that always boosts my faith in God's care is the Gregory Peck/Christopher Plummer film, *The Scarlet and the Black*, the true story of Monsignor Hugh Flaherty, an Irish priest (he later served in California) who outwitted Hitler's SS to save dozens of lives in occupied Rome. The words that appear on the screen at the very end astound with joy at what God can do in any life, even one given to evil. See for yourself!

Inspiring great friends of God's and saints' lives are available in documentary and slightly-to-greatly fictionalized forms, including animated films for family viewing, and may even occasionally be seen on public or commercial TV or staged live. Actor Leonardo di Fillipis sticks closely to the facts in his exceptional one-man theater performances on saints.[27] And don't overlook inspiring documentaries on topics related to saints, such as the inexplicable healings still continuing at Lourdes, France, where St. Bernadette, then a scruffy little girl, saw Jesus' Mother. Another approved apparition, Fatima in Portugal also involves people who became saints in response to their experiences.

3. Underline Scriptures about divine providence.

In the Psalms, your pen can underscore line after line—such as "Your steadfast love, O Lord, endures forever" (Psalm 138:8), "The Lord is my shepherd: I shall not want" (Psalm 23:1), or "Lord, you will show me the path of life and fill me with joy in your presence" (Psalm 16:11)—that rejoices in God's loving care. In the Old Testament, read entire books such as Daniel or Tobit (also titled Tobias) to steep yourself in the millennia-old Jewish understanding that God provides richly for his friends. In the New Testament, in the words of Jesus, Paul, or other apostles, you can mark beautiful Bible promises and instances of God's provision, such as 2 Corinthians 9:8: "God can multiply his favors among you so that you may always have enough of everything and even a surplus for good works." Some will find comfort in the tender verses about providence from Luke 12:22–31 or Matthew

---

27 See Leonardo di Fillipis productions at www.stlukeproductions.com.

6:30: "Consider the lilies of the field . . ." with the admonition "O weak in faith! . . . Stop worrying . . . Your Father knows that you need [material things]." The famed passage ends with the promise that those who surrender to God, seeking him above all else, will have every material need provided as well.

Note, too, the Book of Acts (Acts of the Apostles), the very title referring to God's providential acts to establish the Church.

4. *Consider putting the Book of Acts into action.*

As you read Acts you may wish to seek from God your personal Pentecost, bringing new faith, deeper surrender, and spiritual power into your life by a closer relationship with the Holy Spirit. On November 29, 1972, Pope Paul VI called this a need "for each one of us," not just personally but to "give life to and sanctify the Church," making a better world for all. Moving deeper into the powerful guidance of the Holy Spirit will deepen your understanding of and reliance on God's providence, and may let you pray for needs more effectively in tongues (a form of contemplative prayer) because it bypasses the intellect. Once you receive this gift, you can use it anytime. Many find praying in tongues is particularly helpful when you either wish to praise God and no human words are adequate or when you want to pray for a need but don't know what to say or ask for, as in complex situations. When you don't know, the Spirit does (Romans 8:26)!

How do you move into this deeper relationship? Prayer can get you there—your own or the prayer of others. Seeking others' prayer, you can turn to believing friends or you might seek out a

Charismatic group in good standing with their bishop[28] and ask them to pray for the mighty wind of the Spirit to blow into your being and empower you to live for God in divine providence.

5. *Memorize one or two Scriptures, and then repeat them often to yourself.*

If you tend to doubt God wants to be on your side, how about choosing from these three:

- "I think thoughts of peace and not of affliction" (cf. Jeremiah 29:11),
- "I have come that you might have life and have it to the full" (John 10:10), or
- "I did not come to condemn the world but to save the world" (cf. John 3:17).

If your needs are always on your mind, maybe you'll resonate to "The Lord is good to those who hope in him" (cf. Lamentations 3:25) or Psalm 23 with its consoling promises that God will care for you the way a good shepherd cares for his lambs.

6. *Imitate many saints with quick little prayers, sometimes pictured as "arrows" or "darts" aimed at the heart of God.*

Using these from time to time over the day creates a kind of ongoing dialogue with God that grows faith. The best one is the

---

28 Among the papal-approved are Renewal Ministries headquartered in Michigan (with TV-radio teachers Ralph Martin, Peter Herbeck, and Sr. Ann Shields) and Southern California Renewal Communities (www.SCRC.org). Find a national information center at www.NSC-CharisCenter.org.

one that comes from your heart. But until the day that wells up, try one of these:

- God, I believe. Help me overcome my doubts.
- Jesus, I trust in you.
- Pray for me, Mary, like you prayed for them at Cana.
- Give me deeper faith.
- Pray for me, St. [Name], to have your kind of faith in God's love and care.

Some of us can't pray to have more faith without invoking St. Gaspare del Bufalo (sometimes anglicized as Casper del Bufalo), who died in 1837. From childhood this exceptional soul surrendered to his particular call to serve God in loving attention to the sick, the needy, the aged, and the stranger as a priest. Nevertheless, he was exceptionally sensitive and timid to the point of being a complete scaredy-cat. He loved God and believed in God's love, but he had a nervous disposition that seemed unable to rest in the arms of providence. Yet, apparently hard-heartedly, God kept setting him down in stressful situations. If you know Italian you can read about his adventures in the outstanding two-part biography by A. Rey. Suffice to say, in scary situation after scary situation, he at least received the grace not to run away shrieking.

Prematurely old from stress by his mid-forties, he is pictured by another Italian biographer, Giuseppe De Libero, as not just physically "frail" but "so nervous and sensitive that the sight of a mouse . . . set him trembling." Yet as he continued to put one quivering foot in front of the other, his surrender, in spite of his fears, permitted God to work in his life to the point that Gaspare ended up one of the greatest saints of the nineteenth—or any—

century for trusting divine providence to the point many would consider madness.

Trying to preach nonviolence and love of enemy in an area where what we would today call the Mafia reigned, he was the repeated target of assassination attempts. In one attempt he knew he was handed a cup of deadly poison, but he felt the honor of his host would be compromised if he refused to drink. Murmuring the Scripture, "They shall drink deadly poison, and it shall do them no harm" (Mark 16:18), he tipped back the cup and drank it all. One of the two priest collaborators who had just given the warning collapsed, trembling. "O ye of little faith," Gaspare grinned and without even a hiccup or pause to consider his weak stomach, he rushed off to preach.

On another occasion a knife-wielding assassin was sent. As the man raised his weapon, Father Gaspare said so tenderly, "My son, wouldn't you like to go to confession?" that the unnerved hit man fled. When still another unsavory character was sent to kill him, the saint, who knew the man's intention, took his "visitor" warmly by the arm and led him into another room, closing the door, providing the perfect opportunity for his own murder. When the door opened it was the killer who had "died"—to his old way of life, one of Gaspare's many "Mafia" converts.

If God could provide all this courage and strength for this born-timid soul, God can provide for you too!

7. Have a prayer time.

Consider it an experiment if this is new to you. Prayer arrows are great because they work anyplace, anytime, but you will find you get a lot of solid growth over time by giving God some regular bit of your day. If your health and fatigue quotient permit, you might get up a little earlier or stay up a little later. If that will just make you tired and cranky, maybe you can find five to ten minutes in your day to read a verse of Scripture, talk to God—even if some days you only complain—or do whatever will increase your belief in God's reality, love, and power.

There are myriad ways to pray. The best kind is the prayer that works, that is, connects *you* to God and/or cements that connection. If you persevere with prayer it will—if you are trying to follow the other tenets of this book—bring you deep into God's provision. Prayer, in fact, is the major way all the saints you have met in this book came to know God well enough to live in divine providence.

8. *"Catch" faith by meeting and mingling with people who are really living it.*

Praying, sharing stories from your encounters with God's providence, being on the lookout for it in the lives of others—whether known live or in books or other media—learning some of God's repeated promises in Scripture to provide for you can each grow your faith. But nothing will position you to grow faith more powerfully than following what saints have taught down the centuries: faith is more caught than taught. For instance, the late Cardinal Leon-Josef Suenens (d. 1996), told the Christophers' Father John T. Catoir[29] that he caught faith from his widowed mother. It was by watching her cope with her husband's loss and their subsequent poverty, testified Suenens, "that I was able to learn the art of living day by day, a truly Christian life."

29 See the interview in Catoir's book *Encounters with Holiness*, 75–93.

More examples:

As a young Polish youth whose saintly faith-filled father died during the Nazi occupation of his homeland, Karol Wojtyla (later to become Pope John Paul II), continued to "catch" God through others, perhaps principally through an unmarried accountant-turned-tailor-for-a-simpler-life Jan Tyranowski (d. 1947), a master of contemplative prayer whose life is being studied as a candidate for official sanctity.

Eve Lavallière (d. 1929) had an abusive father who, when she was eighteen, shot and killed her mother in front of her before turning the gun on himself. After going a long way down the wrong roads morally, Eve discovered Christ through a pestering parish priest who wouldn't give up on the famous early-twentieth-century French actress even when she put him in a fury at times. Through this mentor, Eve finally caught faith and was led to a fervent Christian life.

Another who got off to a rocky start was an impoverished Canton, Ohio, Italian-American girl whose dad had early abandoned his toddler and his emotionally unstable wife. Looked down on by "good Catholics" in the 1940s as a child of divorce, young Rita Rizzo caught faith by discovering God's loving providence through a convert laywoman. Rhoda Wise[30] (d. 1948) was on fire with love for God and had experienced two incredible healings during after-death appearances of St. Thérèse of Lisieux sent as God's messenger. Encouraged by Rhoda, teenage Rita made a novena for her prayers to St. Thérèse and was cured of a serious gastrointestinal problem. Realizing that God loved and cared for her, turned Rita into

---

30 See Sources under Rhoda.

Mother Angelica, divine providence's instrument for creating the world's largest TV-radio empire.

One of my friends, Joan Englander,[31] is a living example of the universal benefits of seeking out those who are really living for God. As a young, lapsed Jewish, spiritual seeker, she visited India for six months in 1975–76 searching for spiritual light. She found it in a number of people of different spiritual traditions devoted to God, including some Hindu holy people and Mother Teresa. The living reality of God she returned with led Joan to a life of service to the aged—their gift from divine providence— culminating in her important book *Joy in the Evening of Our Lives: Nurturing the Elderly Soul*[32] while her material needs have been met providentially for years.

People rooted in God can be found without going to India, if you pray and search. Look for them among those staying late to fold chairs after some church or synagogue event or patiently listening to someone who is bereaved, ill, or depressed. Or—the extroverts—quietly without ego heading or working hard for philanthropic groups or events that benefit our human family.

Besides choosing to spend time around people whose lives are truly guided and lived for God (vow to not compare yourself to any of them), you can grow faith in the company of others seeking to do the same thing. If you're no Mother Cabrini, whose holiness and particular "call" let her sweep into town and immediately connect with people, finding seekers like yourself

31 Conversations with the author over the years. Her book *Joy in the Evening of Our Lives: Nurturing the Elderly Soul* (Healing River Press, 2008) is available at www.joanenglander.com.

32 Not written to any one religion, the premise, that elderly people need spiritual and psychological, not just physical, care, is a universal truth.

may not happen overnight. It once took me several years in a new place. But spiritual companions will be found if you pray and keep looking. It is the very rare friend of his that God's divine providence lets end up without spiritual companionship, since this kind of friendship is an important part of most spiritual paths.

That did happen—whether by God's will or something implacable in his personality—in the case of Bl. Charles de Foucauld. A hermit in the desert who enjoyed wonderful relations with the Muslim tribesmen he lived alongside, his extreme austerity drove away any who thought of joining him as spiritual companions. Still, you can take heart even from the case of Charles. For alone in those wastes, Charles' writings show clearly that he was companioned by God himself.

CHAPTER *Five*

Run! Avoid Faith-Killers

W ORKING TO GROW YOUR FAITH IN DIVINE PROVIDENCE
will be hampered, even perhaps squashed, if you
spend an equal amount or more time with faith-killers. The
"post-Christian" world is full of films, other visual and audio
media, including "news" stories on your car radio, on the web,
on your nightly local TV news, or in written media, such as
news magazines and newspapers, books (both fictional and
nonfictional), music, even sometimes art that throw acid at faith.
As you wouldn't ask to be inoculated with leprosy bacillus, why
fill your being with these poisons?

Perhaps the worst poison of all is opting, if you have a
choice, to spend time with people who see existence as ugly
and bleak and spread cynicism, doubt, or the helpless/hopeless
syndrome wherever they go. These may be people who have no
belief in God and even think such belief is foolishness. Why risk
contagion? Be smart. Avoid them.

Am I saying just hang out with church people because they
are the only good people? Not at all. There are true friends of

God who will never be found in churches for varied reasons. And among those who kill joyful trust in divine providence are some in every faith who consider themselves "devout" and are quite unaware of all the mean things they do, sometimes explicitly in God's name, sometimes not, but always with a comfortable sense of their superiority.

For example, besides his fellow porter and biographer, Brother Leo Wollenweber, Father Solanus Casey at times worked with another Capuchin porter who regularly made fun of Solanus' faith-driven attitudes and actions. Happily, Solanus' faith had become so deep that the sneers and derision just rolled off. If you aren't of his spiritual magnitude, consider voluntarily spending time with such people as willfully placing yourself in a cloud of plague-bearing mosquitoes. To put it another way, take care of your interacting, tripartite being of soul-mind-body (I'm quoting early Desert Father St. Antony)[33] by avoiding those who can wear down, even ruin, the health of all three. At least until you are so light-filled your very presence destroys darkness!

PROTECTING YOUR FAITH

Am I asking you—someone is wondering about now—to turn your back on poor unhappy people, and human suffering? Give me a few paragraphs before answering that, because what I am going to say needs some information behind it to be well

---

33 Find the words of the early saint (d. circa 356) in *Early Fathers from the Philokalia*, trans. E Kadloubovsky and G.E.H. Palmer (Faber and Faber, 1954), 31. He is also referred to as Antony (or Anthony) the Abbot.

understood. For starters, let's return to all the media content—film, book, whatever, from the fictional all the way to things as (sometimes only allegedly) factual as a documentary filled with deeply suffering miserable people. Those of us trained journalistically, for instance, know well how a so-called documentary can present partial facts or even untruth regarding some particular kind of suffering to further an agenda. When what is before you—let's turn to fiction here—emerges from someone's deeply jaundiced, perhaps embittered view of life, you are being presented an alternative worldview to the one you are trying to understand and live. Why steep yourself in some miserable script or book writer's life vision of unhappy people battling meaningless suffering?

Avoiding this may *for a time* cause you a problem if you want to be "up on" the latest bestselling books or films or TV programs "everyone" is talking about. (Certainly not all bestsellers or successful programs have this dark view by any means; some are completely wholesome and will grow your faith.) If you are serious about growing faith, the world of eternal supranatural realities and the contrived, unreal world of spiritually immature writers, producers, and other creative people are going to collide inside you. This is inevitable, because however good and well meaning the people who create media filled with misery may personally be, they simply don't perceive the third part of their tripartite nature, the soul, and all the realities that surround its existence.

If instead, you continue on the path to positioning yourself to live in divine providence, your eyes will gradually open to the beauty and truth not just of the world you see but of the equally real world you are immersed in that you see only by its effects, above all divine providence. When supernatural realities are left out in presentations of suffering, you will see "the king has no clothes." And you will have an increasing dislike of putting into your being the false nutrition, in terms of growing faith, of views of life where meaning and growth in suffering are "lucky breaks," not grace and choices. So to answer the question at last, there is no recommendation here that you turn your face away from true human suffering. However, perhaps you would do yourself and others a favor by having the humility to do this for a time.

One way that St. Thérèse of Lisieux demonstrated and grew her holiness was by voluntarily spending time with another nun so cranky all the other nuns avoided her. Thérèse, acclaimed by a pope "the greatest saint of modern times," was a spiritual genius whose faith was already at the heroic level. Most of us can make no claim to be at that level, and I, for one, know from personal experience that trying to help a deeply needy person before you have the necessary spiritual maturity may end up by your hurting them instead, thereby adding guilt and shame to your own emotional and spiritual load.

Beginners in the spiritual life may even have to avoid voluntary knowledge of some sufferings until strong enough to bear them. Let holy Dutch Protestant Casper ten Boom explain what I mean. The watch salesman was on a local train one day with one of his innocent little daughters. Corrie, who later authored that faith-growing book about her holy family's rescue of Jews in World War II, *The Hiding Place*,[34] had heard something, and she wanted her dad to explain to her what the term "sex sin" meant.

---

34 See Sources on the Saints.

In answer Casper took down from overhead his heavy case filled with watches and watch parts and asked, "Will you carry it?" Corrie tried but had to confess, "It's too heavy." "Yes, and I'd be a poor daddy if I asked you to carry it." Then he explained that knowing about some things could also be too heavy for children. "When you are older and stronger," he assured her, she could bear what she couldn't now. So as a little girl, Corrie did not learn the details of sexual sins, because she simply hadn't strength for such a burden. Similarly, if you are trying to become a person of faith in divine providence, you may have to avoid news photos of atrocities, "continuous coverage" of disasters, maybe even the nightly news itself—or many other things that will vary according to your particular weaknesses—until you can see all the sorrows and tragedies of the world with the eyes of faith and a heart that trusts in God.

When there was no food for two or three hundred men in a tragic time, Solanus Casey could have looked at the old and weak, the young and despairing and been dragged into their hopelessness. But he was steeped in the world of faith, not the dismal daily news of this dark era. From his rootedness in divine providence, he looked at each man with faith that God would provide. And God did. You may be sure that when you are stronger spiritually you will—if and as God calls you in your particular case—be able to:

- *Succor the dying* (picture Mother Teresa tenderly picking maggots off a dying woman thrown away like garbage).
- *Sacrifice that others may have justice* (picture Dorothy Day at age seventy-five with a failing heart getting up at 2 AM so

she could be in line to go to jail with Mexicans working as stoop labor under the merciless central California sun and aerial pesticide sprays, in order that these fellow-Catholics and humans might gain more humane working conditions).

- *Bear terrible sorrows* (picture Bl. Zélie Martin in a mother's agony, holding her desperately sick five-year-old Hélène in her arms until the little girl dies, and having the spiritual and emotional strength to give that precious life to God in trust that he has received her).

- *Have untold depths of charity* (picture Dorothy Day again when the father of her child called her thirty years after refusing to marry her, asking her to come care for his woman dying of cancer because he can't cope; Dorothy goes and sees her replacement to her death—and, by the woman's request, into the Catholic church—with neither illusions about her long-ago common-law husband nor resentment).

- *Be God's pillar of strength even in the most bestial captivity* (picture St. Maximilian Kolbe, battered from a beating meant to kill him, tenderly and fearlessly hearing confessions, an act punishable by death, holding to his heart a fellow Auschwitz prisoner. The man spews out terror and hate. When he finally runs down, Kolbe softly counsels, "Love is the only creative response to suffering").

- *Support others in the day-to-day agonies of life* (picture Solanus hour after hour listening to the desperately sorrowful, the terribly ill, those caught up in tragedies, for as long as he was needed to pour God's light—and often physical healing if that was the problem—into their darkness. And doing it even though there were moments when the only way he could bear the monotony of some negative litanies was to keep his heart focused on Christ's patience in his Passion).

Yes, you will do whatever particular part of all this, or other forms of service, you are called to for your family, your neighbor, your community when your surrender has let God turn you, like St. Gaspare, from weak to strong beyond belief.

But if for now you need to take in what one day you will give out, be aware that accepting that humbly is a very wise course.

CHAPTER *Six*

Cultivate Gratitude

NOTHING SO POSITIONS YOU TO LIVE IN GOD'S PROVIDENCE as gratitude.

Holy Claretian Father Aloysius Ellacuria told Charles Carpenter, a young man he eventually inspired to become a priest, "I never deserved any of the graces God gave me. However, when God gave me *any* grace, even small favors, I thanked him with all my heart. And whenever I thanked him, he gave me more graces. So I am convinced that if we are grateful to the almighty God he will give us many, many graces."

Father Solanus was also deeply desirous to pass on the importance of gratitude to all he counseled. "Gratitude," he said, "is the surest sign of intelligence . . . To know God is to be grateful . . . Let us thank God all the time . . . Thank God [even] ahead of time." We do that, taught Solanus, because if our own fear and sadness don't frustrate God's plans, "those plans are always for the best, always wonderful," making gratitude reasonable whether we've received what we need yet or not.

Here are a few ways to cultivate gratitude:

1. *Make a decision to start noticing all the huge gifts you take for granted.*

You could begin, for instance, by thanking God for the ability to move and the ability to breathe.

2. *Make another decision to start noticing all the small gifts of God you receive each day.*

That might mean a slice of buttered toast, sunshine-polished leaves, a stranger's smile on a gray day, a telephone call from a friend, that person who holds the door at the post office when you're laden with packages. Dorothy Day's diary is rich with references to such daily blessings.

3. *Make thanking God part of your daily routine.*

Father Aloysius said he made it a habit to interiorly "constantly" pour out "praise, adoration, love, and *thanksgiving*." Mother Angelica of EWTN fame and her cloistered nuns in Alabama pray four to five hours a day with one hour set aside "for the purpose of thanking him [Jesus] for the marvelous things he does for all mankind." Few have the time for an hour of thanking God, but there are ways to still thank God regularly.

Some families while saying daily grace ask each child, "What are you most grateful for today?" If it works for kids, it works for adults too. If you aren't a grace-saying person, you can tie a little thanksgiving to some regular activity, such as turning on your car for the trip to work or setting your alarm at night. One person I know thanks God for another day of life upon waking up. The point is that if it becomes part of your routine, giving

thanks will be less apt to be something you do enthusiastically—
once or twice—and then forget.

4. *Start a gratitude notebook.*

If you take this route to grow your gratitude, don't make it a
chore or an occasion for guilt. It isn't necessary that you write
every day, that you write everything you have to be grateful
for—to be absurd, imagine trying to put down every breath or
body movement even if you are grateful for those abilities. It
isn't even necessary that you write down the big things God
does for you for which you were so grateful at the moment.
God knows your gratitude; you aren't keeping a gratitude journal for God but to help yourself. Grab the notebook when the
spirit moves you and write whatever comes to mind that you
see as a gift of God: *The utility will work with me to pay the heat-
ing bill. God sent a singing bird to cheer me up. The check came at last.
The blood test didn't hurt.* Later as you read this back, your overall attitude of gratitude will almost certainly increase as you
read about things you may already have forgotten. If you never
read it back, the act of writing with its accompanying focus on
God's gifts and providence will already have helped imprint
gratitude into your being.

5. *Image gratitude.*

Maybe you're not bookish. Twentieth-century Catholic
mystic-artist-writer Caryll Houselander (d. 1954) proposed an
exercise for those who are helped more by images than words.
She suggested pausing from time to time during the day and

envisioning two great hands open in giving with the thought, "At this moment God is handing me all I have."[35]

6. *Ponder how far, in their conviction of the goodness of God, saints take gratitude.*

Hard as it is to believe, Dutch priest Titus Brandsma wrote a poem of love and gratitude to God in a Nazi prison cell. Corrie ten Boom evidenced gratitude for her concentration camp experience that killed her beloved sister.

There was a time in the long life of Father Solanus Casey when, trying to get relief from the misery of chronic eczema on his legs, using someone's "home remedy" backfired so severely, he spent nine weeks in the hospital, much of it in awful pain. He was glad for this time "alone with God" and repeatedly thanked God for the good health God had given him in the past and would be giving him in the future. Back at the friary, still limping around, Solanus wrote his brother James that a number of his friends in and outside the hospital thought he had had a "close call," but he himself never thought that. Then writing about himself in the third person, he told James, "It seemed about ten days of the really best penance that the poor sinner Solanus had ever gone through. Therefore, since by God's grace he persevered and lived through it without complaint, we have a reason to thank God for the wonderful experience." Meditating on such incidents—even for those of us who can't yet emulate them—is growth-producing!

---

35 Joyce Kemp, *The Spiritual Path of Caryll Houselander* (Paulist Press, 2001), 112.

7. *Show concretely you are grateful for divine providence by giving God a little something in thanks.*

Sometime after Catherine de Hueck's [later Doherty's] father's pre-1918 Revolution death in Russia, her mother discovered squirreled away in the farthest reaches of his desk a little notebook. It revealed the businessman had, unbeknown even to his family, provided university educations to a number of needy youngsters. He noted each scholarship was an act of gratitude to God for many blessings.

Most people can't do so much, but the amount, or that it involve money, is not important. Saints living in poverty, such as Thérèse of Lisieux, Bl. Titus Brandsma (in that Nazi prison), Mother Teresa of Calcutta, and Father Solanus Casey, let their gratitude spill over into poetry. In addition, in one friary where Solanus lived, it is recalled that each Sunday night the gray-garbed, rail-thin friar would play his violin in the empty chapel for Jesus in the Tabernacle. Gently, Solanus urged some of his visitors, too, to do something for God, not just ask him for favors. He suggested certain things, according to a Capuchin biographer, because he knew God wants everyone to know him and his ways better. To some barely committed "Christmas and Easter Catholics," he suggested attending Mass regularly; to those who worshiped every Sunday, he might suggest one weekday Mass if they could fit that in; a not-so-regular Protestant might be asked if she could promise to get to her church each Sunday.

Sometimes Solanus suggested the person seeking a favor of divine providence promise God something in return if the request were granted as the petitioner desired. It was never a huge commitment—Solanus didn't want to see anyone make a promise too hard to keep—and it was always aimed at helping the petitioner know God or his providence better. A man who came seeking help for ulcers admitted he hadn't been to church since his wedding twenty-one years earlier. Aghast that anyone would try to live without God's help, Solanus exclaimed, "Why don't you go in and kneel and thank God you're still walking after all these years! No wonder you have ulcers! Now, if you promise me right now you will go to confession and go to Communion, your health will be returned. Will you do that?" The man said he would.

Father Solanus had him kneel, blessed him, and shot him right off to confession (as a simplex priest he couldn't hear confessions but he always asked the priests who heard his visitors to not scold and to be "good to them"). In this case the man told another Capuchin, "I never had any pain after I saw Father Solanus."

Others were asked to promise that if they were healed they would do some other spiritual act: having a Mass said for someone in need, enrolling someone in what is today called the Capuchin Mission Mass Association (those two meant a very small donation for the missions and were a chance to grow faith by seeing providence in action), or reading a spiritual book.

Maybe you could do a little something for God. Just remember: don't go overboard with a commitment too big to keep. God won't punish you any more than you would punish your little child who exclaims, "I love you; I'm gonna build you a castle!" but why mix that spoonful of guilt into your gratitude cup?

8. *Make a decision that you will react with gratitude for what
   you have, the moment you notice you are down about what
   your life lacks, even if you have to search hard for a glimmer
   of light in encircling darkness.*

The letters from sisters Corrie and Betsie ten Boom in Nazi
captivity, even taking into consideration that they wouldn't have
been sent if they told it like it was, show genuine attitudes of
looking for those glimmers of light and focusing on them. And
Corrie's smuggled-out uncensored writings both tell of cruelties
to her and others and show her determination, with the help
of divine providence, to push through soul-chilling events and
sights to rejoice in God's company.

Call it a list; call it a litany. On the morning you wake
up overwhelmed by your situation, before you can sink in
that slough, say, "I'm going to think of five (you'll know the
number) things I can be grateful for." Now say them mentally
or jot them down. In theory this may require great struggle.
Actually even just looking to your body, some things work or
you wouldn't have awakened, right? And the sun came up. You
get the picture. Do this on-the-spot list as a habit, and you will
find it easier and easier to think of more things going right,
working, or coming your way. You may eventually be able to
rattle off fifty or a hundred causes for gratitude even when
you have financial or business issues, health issues, or personal
relationship issues all at the same time. Of course, it is not the
number that is important. It is turning your mind away from
drowning helplessly and hopelessly in the sea of your troubles
to reach out for God's saving hand—a simple change of focus

that, like storm clouds unexpectedly opening to reveal the sun, can raise your eyes to God's providence.

A hurting person once said to me, "But what if you are homeless without a bed? What do you thank God for then?" I know from their lives that Father Solanus and Father Aloysius, or any holy person, would help the homeless person rather than preach to him. But I believe if counsel were also sought, Father Solanus would encourage you, if this book has come into your hands while you are bunking with relatives, sleeping in your car, refuged in a shelter or on the street from economic or natural disaster, like the author at various times from fire and flood, to thank God for the borrowed bed, the bedroll, the shelter, or the cardboard box. And if you have none of these, to thank God for life itself. I believe Father Solanus would add, thank God, trustingly, for the time when you will again have a bed of your own the way Solanus, hospitalized in terrible pain, thanked God for his *future* health.

So, whether you are (God forbid) in a box on the street or in your own or a borrowed comfortable bed, on a night you can't sleep from focusing on your economic or other worries or pain, lying there instead picturing all you *can* be grateful to God for is better than a sedative. Recent studies, in fact—with no reference to God and the blessings thanking him brings—claim the act of gratitude all by itself increases serotonin and dopamine levels, body chemicals associated with "pleasure and contentment."[36] So on those bad nights start thanking God interiorly for each

36 University of California, Davis, Professor Robert A. Emmons' interview with writer David Hochman in the article "Just Say Thanks," *Reader's Digest* (November 2009): 144.

of your blessings, and even science confirms you'll likely drift peacefully to sleep on this wave of thanksgivings.

CHAPTER *Seven*

Retool Your Mind

A NGELA BOUDREAUX OF NEW ORLEANS WENT TO HER DOCTOR in 1966 with a liver nine times normal size. Biopsies found many malignant cells and surgery was scheduled in Southern Baptist Hospital without delay.

CONSIDER FATHER FRANCIS SEELOS

Some time before this, Angela's youngest son had received healing when she trustingly requested the prayers of one of God's friends, Father Francis Xavier Seelos, who was buried at St. Mary's Assumption Church. Turning again for prayer support to the priest, whose reputation for holiness had never dimmed, Angela put herself in the divine hands. The Protestant surgeon was willing to pin a relic of Father Seelos to his operating cap—Angela, as the patient, could not wear it—as a sign of Angela's request for the nineteenth-century Redemptorist's prayer intercession.

It would seem the intercession was not forthcoming. The operation revealed a liver 90 percent "replaced" by a huge malignant tumor. Her doctor told Angela she'd be dead in two weeks. Her close blood relatives had all died of cancer, but she did not slump in her chair, helpless and hopeless. Angela—who would later describe herself to this author as "a very positive thinker"—asked instead, "How are you going to treat me?"

The startled physician answered *if* she were alive in two weeks, fifteen doctors across the country would confer on what to do. He didn't add "for a hopeless case."

Two weeks later Angela was not only alive, her liver was improving, which it did until all the tests—and its huge size—were once again normal. On her way home from the hospital, although warned not to kneel so soon after surgery, she made a stop at Father Seelos' grave in the Irish Channel district and knelt to thank God and him for the cure she was sure was in progress.

She was eventually given some chemo, a derivative of the mustard gas that had devastated WWI soldiers. She, however, had no ill effects. The doctor—like the surgeon also a non-Catholic—would testify that this chemo never cured anyone *and* that Angela's inexplicable cure was well underway by the time she was treated.

Angela had a well-tooled mind—surrendered, grateful, and expectant—to receive God's providence. She received it in the form of a cure that astounded her doctors at Southern Baptist and was eventually accepted as the official beatification miracle for Father Seelos. A thrilled Angela took part in Francis Xavier Seelos' beatification at St. Peter's in April 2000.[37]

---

37 For more details of her incredible faith, see Sources on the Saints under Francis Xavier Seelos.

Angela demonstrates a mind that lives divine providence down to its core.

The whole question of who is healed and who isn't being a true mystery, I am not making the simplistic claim that Angela Boudreaux received a miracle because she was either a positive thinker or because of her incredible trust in divine providence—miracles have gone to people with no faith whatsoever; but I will say whatever had happened—even had she died at that time instead of almost forty years later—Angela would have fared better because of her *faith* in God's loving providence that blocked agitation and let God work.

Few of us can avoid all agitation and trust God's providence to the degree Angela Boudreaux did. In fact, to move toward what we can call the divine providence-permeated lifestyle, the average mind needs a bit, to a lot, of retooling *in its depths* to cast out the negative and welcome more of God's light.

Here, once again, are some specific techniques toward the goal. There are so many found in saints' lives that are effective, for someone if not everyone, that I can't begin to offer them all. If you don't find any of my picks in this or the next chapter helpful, read intensively among the lives of the saints with an eye out for how each of them "retooled." First is the one I deem most essential:

1. *Uncover and study your mental script.*

If this seems very hard, ask God to reveal it to you. God being a gentleman, as Malibu, California, Episcopal priest Rex Broyles used to insist in his St. Aidan's sermons, it is extremely unlikely you are going to come face-to-face with the whole script at one blow. But if you ask God, sincerely wanting to grow, I can promise you that you will gradually see or hear, depending upon how your mind works, the endless inner patter, the inner slogans and precepts and the little ongoing fantasies you live by, normally without much if any awareness. You may discover one day in prayer, as I did some years back, that a lot of what is going on just below ordinary consciousness is shockingly negative.

You may be aghast to uncover, for instance, a steady stream of negativity in regard to how others are going to react to you, perceive your intentions, the probable outcome of your efforts, or whether God desires to help you. You may find you have a surprisingly critical view of others, or of yourself, or discover below your consciousness an archive of wrongs done to you that you haven't forgiven.

NEGATIVE SCRIPTS

With God's help you can catch yourself each time one of your negative scripts pops up, roundly reject it, and replace it with something positive. For example, if you go into every job interview with inner whispers of, "They'll never hire me," the second you become aware of that voice, you can retort, "Why wouldn't they hire me? I'm a competent, hardworking person and I have a great attitude."

If it's too hard to go in so positive—a fair number of people have actually been conditioned that God will knock you down if you expect good things or say anything nice, however truthful, about yourself—how about just saying the positive things you dare to, perhaps the modest "I have the skills to do this job." Retool your dialogue to at least say each time, "Something good will come out of this interview." Again, this is not the power of positive thinking, although I am not knocking that—it beats the opposite by a mile—but a retooling into trust that God will fulfill his promise that, for those who want to be God's friends, all things will eventually work out for good (Romans 8:28).

If you have been raised or learned along the way to avoid disappointment by always expecting the worst, retool that thinking as best you can, *as fast as you can*, because all by itself that is a huge umbrella between you and the rain of God's endless mercies and material supply. Tell yourself that you can live through disappointments if they happen (after all, by the time you hit kindergarten, you'd had a gazillion of them, from being weaned to the other kid getting the red tricycle), but meantime you are going to gain all the joy and other benefits, mental, spiritual, and physical, that come by being expectant of good. Or, as Father Solanus put it, "In fostering confidence we greatly eliminate the danger of sadness that frustrates God's merciful designs."

Perhaps you absorbed early the dictum that only perfection will do. As a result, some just-below consciousness voice is always scolding you. It is hard to accept God's providence if you think it's only for the "perfect."

A reminder: God's saints aren't perfect, just surrendered.

G.K. Chesterton left all of us who suffer from perfectionism a wonderful dictum: "Anything worth doing is worth doing badly."

Consider also the old Italian proverb (sometimes incorrectly attributed to Voltaire because he quoted it), "The perfect is the enemy of the good."

If any of the inner mental patterns just mentioned—fearing God's displeasure if you succeed and are happy, clutching negative expectations to avoid disappointment, constantly feeling too imperfect to warrant God's providence, or scrupulously aiming at perfection—are deeply embedded, don't be afraid to get help from either an emotionally and spiritually mature spiritual director (ideally a priest for Catholics who can help you through the sacrament of Reconciliation as well) or an emotionally and spiritually mature psychotherapist. The cost can be affordable if you seek out places that charge on a sliding scale; there are also a few places that will provide help free to sincere seekers. God's providence can work in wondrous ways through such people.[38]

Just be sure anyone you consult is truly a man or woman who knows by experience God's reality, love, power, and desire to help you retool. Being ordained doesn't automatically guarantee this. For instance, I once heard a learned psychiatrist-priest assert that those brought up by very strict or abusive fathers would never be able to relate to God the Father. He obviously didn't understand about the transformation that takes place as you invite God into your life. I wish I could introduce him to a woman I've known for decades in Spokane, Washington. Although her father beat and did terrible things to her, Sandra Lee bubbles over with joy in God the Father and his amazing

---

38 If neither is an option, try to get hold of a copy of the book *Prayer Can Change Your Life* by William R. Parker and Elaine St. Johns.

providence to her. Your past father or other wounds *can* be healed by God, too, but obviously you won't want to look for help with your cure to someone who believes a transformation such as Sandra's is impossible.

The priest who didn't know that God completely retools those who surrender to him (see Scriptures such as Romans 12:2 or 2 Corinthians 5:17) reminded me of my one visit back in college with the campus psychiatrist, the deadest-looking alive man I ever saw. He proved to be an atheist whose only answer to my perfectionism was the absolutely unhelpful—because I couldn't do it just for wishing—"lower your standards." He went on to kill himself, and I went on to be healed through God's retooling love—a mystery of mercy I pray he shared en route to the other side. Obviously you don't want "help" growing your faith from someone who has none.

While the most important thing you can do to retool, I believe, is to journey with God into the inner workings of your mind, here are auxiliary things able to help the process along:

2. *Give God time and the opportunity to heal your anger and/ or sadness in areas where you question divine goodness or have a personal grudge against God.*

Hard as it may be to believe, your feelings and view can radically change given time and openness to God. Take WWII Holocaust survivor, author, and Jewish spirituality expert Rolf Gompertz, for instance. Rolf shared with me that one day he realized that the bitter, angry question, "Where was God?" actually should be "Where was humanity?" It was not God, he saw, but people choosing evil, and those who didn't stop them, who murdered members of his family not able to escape as he and his parents had. Although I am not Jewish, from my late childhood, I worried whether God could be good in a world where millions were slaughtered for their ethnicity. Gradually, I too discovered that people created the Holocaust and found in my researches time and again[39] that God was with its victims. With awe, I realized good had triumphed—Hitler perished while the new state of Israel rose from the ashes and the Jewish people continued their unique role in human spirituality. Far from my roadblock to faith in a good God, the survival of the Jewish people is now a pillar of that faith.

In a more personal vein, my child's cancer brought deep sadness but I had to eventually acknowledge, too, that it was not God but exposure to toxins that caused it. If God permitted this, God was with us obviously on most days and on a few others in ways hard to see then but less obscure in retrospect. What is crystal clear years later is that God brought good out of the whole for my daughter. Now a mother herself, she says of the horrible experience, she would never want to go through it again, but she is grateful for the way cancer at fourteen changed her values and thus her life.

Of course, my life, and maybe yours, echoes Padre Pio's when he said, "I am a mystery to myself." Some sufferings even decades later remain inexplicable. Did God just permit this terrible thing or was it *sent* for my and/or another's growth? What giving God time and a chance can achieve in these hard instances has come for me to be epitomized by my faith-filled Protestant, Swedish immigrant grandmother. The last time

---

39 See, for example, Yaffa Eliach, *Hasidic Tales of the Holocaust*, Oxford University Press, 1982 and, on three secular Jews, see fn #51, p. 126.

I saw her, she lay paralyzed on one side, as she had been for several years. Yet the face turned up to me was not just smiling but lit by some inner glow as she said serenely to my unasked question, "We'll understand all this some day." A lifetime of sincerely letting God in can eventually let us live peacefully and trustingly the unsolved mysteries of our lives.

3. *Use some of those Scriptures you memorized to replace negative inner maxims as you become aware of them.*

I mean things such as "Life is a jungle," "Everybody's out to get me," "Nobody cares about me," or "I just don't have what it takes."

To the Scriptures you already know you could add new ones. One recommended to a woman dominated by fear of death by St. Frances de Sales (d. 1622)[40] is "O God, who has ever trusted in thee and been put to shame?" (Sirach 2:10 or Ecclesiasticus. 2:11). If your maxims come from any kind of fear, even if you don't know what you are afraid of precisely, that verse could work for you. If negative maxims pop up as you struggle with decisions, try repeating the counsel of the book of Proverbs (3:6), with a twist: "I'll acknowledge you, God, in all my ways and you shall direct my paths."

4. *Check your prayer practices for any need to retool.*

Could you actually be praying negatively? Here's an example of a negative prayer: "Help me, Lord, to bear having no money to pay the light bill. The kids are so afraid of the dark. I ask you again to forgive my sin of cursing last week that has turned

---

40 De Sales was known for his gift of counsel, and his books of wise advice for ordinary people seeking God are still read today.

you against us." When you ask for forgiveness, accept it! There truly is no need to keep asking to be forgiven for the same act. Catholics who can use the sacrament of Reconciliation should. Then fling whatever it was into the abyss of God's mercy. And get this straight: God, who always wants your good, doesn't turn against anyone; people turn against God. Moreover, asking God to help you bear having no money nine times out of ten is a way of affirming there is no divine providence. Ask God for the money you need!—and to heal your children. Get the kids praying too, for income and for freedom from fear. God will provide! But divine providence will find it hard going if you keep praying negatively instead of expectantly.

Prayer Can Change Your Life by college professor-psychologist and prayer expert Dr. William R. Parker is great on the types of prayer that actually close you off from God and from retooling and teaches its opposite: how to pray in a way that allows God to help you.[41] Dr. Parker chides, "What finer evasion can we use than to say it's God's will that we suffer greatly in this world and [we] are not required to do anything about those things we could change?"

Along those lines, make sure that you aren't caught up in a swamp of *pious* negativity. We do this when we not only expect to have everything go badly, but we take pride in it, even holding so tightly to the concept of suffering here and reward in heaven that, if God came to the door offering relief from burdens, a way would be found to refuse the offer. A few may carry this so far as to live in a little fantasy of being a special victim soul.

41 *Prayer Can Change Your Life: Experiments and Techniques in Prayer Therapy* by William R. Parker and Elaine St. Johns (Prentice-Hall, 1957), 42–46, 128, 171. The book is still available for purchase for good reason: it teaches effective prayer.

Having studied genuine, and not genuine, victim souls for several decades now, I have a few words for you. I am convinced if you want (even a little bit) to be a victim soul, especially if you find in yourself some feeling of "specialness" about it, there's a huge chance what's happening is not of God. Bl. Alexandrina da Costa (d. 1955), St. Padre Pio, and beatification candidate Theresa Neumann (d. 1962) are wonderful examples of the genuine article, and none of them felt "special" or desired to serve God *in this particular way.*

Twentieth-century Portuguese laywoman Alexandrina da Costa, eventually invalided after she beat would-be rapists off two other young women and then jumped out a high window to escape, had a healthy spirituality. Far from desirous to be a bedridden "victim," she spoke for a long time of dancing in the streets when she was cured.

A strong, active young woman who took a man's place in the Bavarian farm fields while WWI swallowed all able-bodied males, Theresa Neumann wanted to go to the missions as a nun. As a youth Pio wanted to serve God; and under Jesus his life would be a battle to save souls, but when he received the stigmata this occasioned no pride in his "special victimhood"; it was instead an enormous humiliation and embarrassment. When ill, Pio also worked toward and prayed for healing. If you feel you are a special victim soul, take courage, and do your best to send such thoughts to the devil, from where they almost assuredly came. The only safe road to God's providence is to cultivate as much faith as you can and be *expectant* for God's bounty. Time enough to do the victim act when God, through circumstances you did nothing to bring about and didn't desire, validated by a truly competent spiritual director, sets you on that rare road of full-time reparatory suffering. Even then down-to-earth good cheer is the purest mark of authenticity.

Servant of God Marthe Robin (d. 1981), paralyzed and blind from age thirty-seven, was a genuine reparatory sufferer. She also lived on the Eucharistic host without eating or drinking anything else. Accused of secretly eating, this French woman showed no indignation, cheerfully agreeing she'd certainly eat if she could, volunteering that she compensated by "imagining menus" and imagining eating with them the foods she sent death-row prisoners. Remembering odors also gave her pleasure, and—unable to move her legs—she looked forward to the day she would dance with joy in heaven. One who knew her speaks of her wonderful laugh.

As we try to retool toward that joy that, as Mother Teresa put it, catches souls for God, it's okay to offer up sufferings[42] (even something like not having money to pay the light bill) for someone in need, maybe your own kids who are frightened of the dark, while praying expectantly for the funds, and, if you have the trust, thanking God ahead of time for them. There's no pious egoism or negativity here; just a commonsense appreciation that nothing should be wasted on the road to plenty.

What else can you do to make yours a more positive prayer? Here are some suggestions from Dr. Parker's book—mixed with some of my own ideas and two suggestions from friends:

---

42 In this old custom, you take what you are suffering and unite it to the sufferings of Christ, so it becomes of more value as a prayer for whomever you "offer" it.

- Let each prayer be an act of *surrender*, hopefully, as much
  as you can, withholding nothing.
- Make prayer an exercise in *honesty* (God knows anyway),
  bringing him your fears, hates, resentments, healthy and
  unhealthy guilt, and all the other stuff you try to hide.
  Far from condemning you, God understands how and
  why you are as you are better than you do and wants to
  help you to freedom.
- Accept God's forgiveness and give it to others.
- Pray *regularly*.
- Be sure you are praying *positively*.
- Give some prayer time to silence, with the intention of
  just letting God love you and speak to your heart.
- Be *receptive* to God's wonderful designs for you.
- Ask God to heal you, body, mind, and soul.
- Then, having asked for healing, as the author's friend
  Father Tom Bill, CSC, puts it: *be expectant!*

5. *Replace with a new positive personal motto any negative one you may have unconsciously been living by.*

Here are two examples of negative mottos: "I'm climbing my
way to the top—so look out the rest of you!" or conversely,
"Stomp on me, world; I deserve it." Ask God and he will give you
a healthier motto, in one way or another, to live by, as he did for
many saints. Three examples:

St. Frances Cabrini: "I can do all things through Christ who
strengthens me" (Philippians 4:13).

St. Maximilian Kolbe: "Love without limits."

Father Solanus: "Thanks be to God," repeated over and over as a litany of gratitude "through every event, every thought of his life."

6. *Consider your name.*

Only some will resonate to this, but I have known a few people who, as they grew spiritually, needed to change the form of their name—an immature Jack becoming the more grown-up John or, conversely, an overly dignified John becoming down-to-earth Jack. Chiara Lubich, for instance, was born Silvia. When she became what was referred to then as a Third Order, that is, lay, Franciscan (today's Secular Franciscans), she took the name Chiara, Italian for Clare.[43] Later, rather than just reserving the name for her Franciscan activities, she adopted it permanently as part of the spiritual transformation that birthed the Focolare Movement.

A new name bespeaking a new life is still a tradition upon entering some religious communities. When Lucien Bunel became Carmelite father Jacques of Jesus, this told the world to whom the future WWII martyr of charity (he hid Jewish boys in the school he headed) wanted to belong and indicated his clean and simple spiritual road. St. Thérèse of the Child Jesus and Bl. Elizabeth of the Trinity (d. 1906) are two other Carmelites whose unique paths to God are seen in their names. Maybe you want to dub yourself with a Carmelite-type name for your private prayer.

---

43 The name change is rare today, American Franciscans say.

These young women, Thérèse and Elizabeth, also are examples of those who discover a phrase—want to ask God for yours?—that sums up an individual's special calling in the kingdom of God, the "secret name" spoken of in many spiritualities. Thérèse said, "I will be love in the heart of the Church." Elizabeth of the Trinity saw herself, from Ephesians 1:6, as "Praise of Glory." For those who are called, this may be a hugely important discovery that plants you in the heart of providence.

7. *Consider using music as an auxiliary retooling device.*

If you are a music lover, you can let this pleasurable activity help you retool. If the music you listen to, for instance, is the kind with lyrics, you can saturate yourself in this easy way with messages that bolster your belief in God and your optimism about God's love and care for you. Beyond lyrics, important studies at Columbia Hospital in New York demonstrate that music all by itself has powerful brain effects. Not the same music affecting everyone but the music—say, for one person Bach, for another Mozart—an individual resonates to. It does not have to be classical music. Other studies at Beth Abraham Hospital, also in New York, prove simply using music someone reacted positively to rewired brains.[44] Most of us who like music

---

44 The scans at the Neurological Institute of New York at Columbia Hospital involved noted neuro-psychiatrist, faculty member, and author Oliver Sacks. Sacks's brain either lit up or went flat in reaction to varied classical music. Beth Abraham Hospital's Institute for Music and Neurologic Function where the second studies were done was cofounded by Dr. Sacks and Concetta Tomaino. These studies involved "music therapy," in which music a patient reacted positively to let paralyzed limbs move or the voiceless speak.

have experienced *that the right music promotes peacefulness*. That state in turn, perhaps even as background to prayer, facilitates emotional and spiritual growth. If you like to sing, retooling that way is possible by taking a tip from the apostle Paul, who recommends that "you sing psalms and hymns and spiritual songs with thankfulness in your hearts to God" (Colossians 3:16). If you are involved with music that promotes negative thoughts and feelings, make a decision to turn toward more wholesome varieties. Then whatever you listen to, you can make at least some of your music time work enjoyably for your mental uplifting and retooling.

8. *Use the power of repetition.*

If your mind tends to harass you by unceasing litanies of your material or other woes, you can replace these, for brief periods anyway (and perhaps grow the time with practice), by reciting at least a portion of the Rosary, the Divine Mercy Chaplet, a favorite psalm or a single word such as *God* or *Shalom*, or the "Jesus Prayer" from Eastern Orthodoxy ("Lord Jesus Christ, have mercy on me, a sinner").[45] Retooling by gently repeating a "sacred word," such as *God* or *Jesus*, to stave off distractions in the ancient monastic technique today called Centering Prayer will also work for some. If you've been taught that "vain repetition" is displeasing to God, I can refer you to sincere lovers of God who've discovered, as

45 Studies of meditation involving repetition and "the relaxation response" it evokes, described in such books as Kenneth Pelletier's *Mind as Healer, Mind as Slayer*, Jesuit William Johnston's *Silent Music* and *The Mirror Mind*, and Episcopalian priest Morton Kelsey's *The Other Side of Silence*, make clear that repetition of the right kind retools.

musician W. Keith Moore did, that "repetitious prayer is only vain if your attitude allows it to be." The musician says that in spite of his misgivings, spending days frequently repeating the Jesus Prayer retooled his mind. He says, "My desire for Jesus grew" so much that his goal now is to become a saint.[46]

Saying other memorized prayers such as the *Our Father*—recommended, after all, by Jesus himself when asked for instruction in how to pray—should not be overlooked either, on the grounds that one says them time and again: Jesus appears to have definitely meant the *Our Father* to be used as a mainstay of communication with God. Moreover, if you ponder the teachings within the *Our Father* (even just addressing God as "Father" can change your view of humanity) as you say it, hopefully slowly, you are saturating your being with the reality view of Jesus Christ. It is not a great leap to think that he taught this prayer in order that repeating it mindfully would gradually transform its users. The same may be urged of the beautiful *Shema*, Israel's most important prayer, that many devout Jews say twice a day.

Certain prayers, said once a day or more often, can become powerful agents for renewal—for moving from mental darkness to light—when used mindfully with positive intent. And be sure they do some good even when said mindlessly out of habit, if only by replacing negative mental patter.

9. *Give special thought to bedtime.*

What you put into your mind at bedtime before turning out the light can be a powerful retooler. A few minutes reading short

46 From his conversion testimony found at http://chnetwork.org/2011/07 /keeping-jesus-at-the-center-w-keith-moore/.

teachings, prayers, poems, and/or litanies by the saints and the saintly are all good. For instance, when people gathered about Mother Teresa as if she were a celebrity, she handed out what she called her "business card." On it were words one could ponder before sleep:

> The fruit of silence is prayer
> The fruit of prayer is faith
> The fruit of faith is love
> The fruit of love is service
> The fruit of service is peace[47]

If you find bedtime spiritual reading either gets your mind too engaged or puts you to sleep immediately, after your usual mystery, crossword puzzle, chat with your spouse, whatever you favor, it might work for you to pass into sleep hearing (using headphones if you are not alone) recorded songs/ hymns, litanies, prayers, or even tapes made specifically for you by yourself, a friend, or a professional, suggesting positive changes to enhance your faith. All these materials can work on the mind's deeper layers, which are more open in sleep. Over time, this can plant more reassurance (for example, in anxious minds that trust divine providence pretty well during the day but not after sundown) than barred windows or triple-locked doors.

---

46 *Love: A Fruit Always in Season: Daily Meditations by Mother Teresa*, Ignatius Press, 1987.

CONSIDER CHARLES DE FOUCAULD

How completely retooled can a mind become, in terms of casting out darkness and being flooded with the light of divine providence? And what does a completely retooled mind look like? Let us examine an early life that, like St. Gaspare del Bufalo, but in completely different ways, revealed great need for retooling: Bl. Charles de Foucauld.

When he was about five, Charles experienced the tragic deaths of his father and his mother, and then—before Charles's very eyes—his only living grandmother, who, taking the by then six-year-old orphan and his three-year-old sister for a walk, was charged by a herd of cows. The grandmother, French Vicomtesse de Foucauld, successfully dragged aside the walking boy and the cart containing the girl and then died of fright.

Charles's mother had been "both virtuous [and] extremely religious." A biographer described her as gliding "dolefully through the household, convinced that life was but one long ordeal intended to make one worthy of heaven." She passed on that kind of faith to her little son; faith that sees life only as an ordeal meted out by a stern God could not sustain such a tragedy, and died with his family. He tried to "behave" but was prone to emotional outbursts.

Once the maternal grandfather, the only grandparent left, who took the children in, died, Charles went wild, using the fortune he inherited to give himself up to the outwardly glamorous, inwardly miserable playboy lifestyle. Educated as a military officer, he was sent home from a colonial post, because he deliberately flaunted his mistress before the officers' wives and daughters.

When war broke out he straightened up out of loyalty to his military mates, was reinstated, and after honorable service, became a noted explorer. Yet always he remained too marked by his early traumas to be easy with spiritual realities. Sudden conversion at age twenty-eight through a saintly priest and a cousin changed all that completely.

His discovery that God was real led him into deep surrender and inner change. So profoundly had he retooled from inner misery to joy in the Lord, that he experienced the highest mystical event possible in this life, the mystical marriage. Charles of Jesus, as he was now called, wanted to live like Jesus in Nazareth, that is, in silent oneness with God without public ministry. But whereas Jesus had all the joys of his mother, Joseph, kin, and neighbors, Charles sought out ever more solitary hermitages. From them he wrote time and again to his spiritual director back in France, "My usual state is pleasure in the presence of Jesus," or, "I am happy very happy."

He would have liked companions to join him as he lived among Muslims in today's Algeria as "their little brother." But his extreme lifestyle attracted no one. He remained alone but in deep companionship with Jesus. In 1916, living in his final hermitage among the Taureg tribe in Algeria's Sahara, he was murdered by anti-French marauders. Then, having died a happy man but, like Jesus, apparently a failure, he was resurrected as a role model for many who try to live out his spirituality. Among thousands of handwritten pages that Charles left is the following prayer, that shows how a traumatized orphan had been utterly retooled into a lavishly loved, lavishly loving and trusting child.

My Father,
I abandon myself to you.
Make of me what you will.
Whatever you make of me,
I thank you.

I am ready for everything.
Provided that your will be done in me,
And in all your creatures,
I desire nothing else, Lord.

I put my soul in your hands,
I give it to you, Lord,
With all the love in my heart,
Because I love you,
And because it is for me a need of love
To give myself,
To put myself in your hands unreservedly,
With infinite trust.
For you are my Father.

Perhaps you *still* wonder whether you can hope for access to divine providence. Absolutely. Charles de Foucauld was a million miles from this prayer when he made the initial leap of surrender.

The first time I heard the prayer of de Foucauld's spiritual maturity, I had surrendered to God as much as I could, and God—who rewards even puny efforts generously—was letting me live materially to a large degree by grace. God did this in spite of the reality that after years of retooling, my trust level was still mediocre: contemplating giving God as much power over my life as the prayer does frightened me. Maybe the thought scares you too.

But keep on surrendering and retooling as you can—*remember it's a process*—with your heart facing Godward and stomping on any worry that you won't get help until you are all the way surrendered or retooled. *You will always get as much as you can accept at the time.* As for me, a decade later the prayer seems beautiful and eminently sensible, while the old fears make me laugh as I experience providence in ever more amazing ways.

Rather than fret that your retooling doesn't yet match the retooling of Gaspare del Bufalo and Charles de Foucauld, boldly ask God to do for you what he did for these men whose lives of anxiety and desperate hedonism, respectively, were completely transformed into joy and trust. And if Charles' spirituality—so extreme, it ended in God permitting a shot to his head as his entry to paradise—scares you, that's unique to him. Be assured St. Gaspare, the untouched survivor of many assassination attempts, died in the pleasant city of Rome in a comfortable bed, men who loved him clustered around. The one-time scaredy-cat faced death with no fear. Witnesses—including one canonized today[48]—noted Gaspare died with such "sweetness" and "peace . . . as if immersed in the joys of paradise," that it awakened one's own desire for death. Oh truly, right to the end God does provide.

---

48 St. Vincent Pallotti.

Practice Belief in God's Providence— Even Fake It When Necessary

W HATEVER FAITH IN GOD'S PROVIDENCE YOU'VE GROWN YOU can strengthen by *practice*—the way you practice any other skill you want to master. Here are seven things you can do:

1. *Practice acting as if you have more faith in divine providence than you do.*

Do this not to impress anyone but because there is something about living like one who strongly believes that helps birth more belief.

St. Thérèse of Lisieux never had more than minimal retooling to do, with her two holy parents and natural spiritual genius. But under the effects of terminal tuberculosis, which brings with it depression of spirit as well as difficulty breathing, she lost her belief in the reality of the life to come. This after spending her life with her eyes upon heaven's glories, engaged in spiritual work in a cloistered Carmel—a Mary at the feet of Christ. If there was, instead, *nothing* to come and God didn't exist, her life had been, to put it mildly, pretty misguided.

Thérèse handled this "dark night" of faith by, as she said, making more formal acts of faith than she had in her entire life. She did not prattle on to others about her state. She acted *as if* she still had faith. In a strange way—the mystics reading this will understand—she still did. This is evidenced by sincere remarks she made such as "I will *come down*" (after death) to fulfill her desire "to work for souls until the end of time."[49]

Her ploy of refusing to accept what her TB-influenced mind was telling her, and countering it with prayerful acts of faith, received the heavenly seal of approval, for just moments before she died her face lit up with ecstasy. What she had longed for, hoped for, and refused to dismiss, no matter what her mind said, appeared to her. God did provide.

The formal Act of Faith Thérèse used, found in any Catholic prayer book, or one of your own, such as, "God, I believe in your reality and loving power," repeated frequently, is one path through murky belief in divine providence.

2. *Thank God ahead of time for meeting your various needs— even if you are only going through the motions and without much hope of receiving what is asked for.*

Do this whether the need is small, such as a parking place, or big, such as mortgage money. A reminder: Following this counsel of Father Solanus to thank God ahead of time is *not* making something come true by your own power through visualizing it (although that can be very useful in physical healing—for

---

49 After her death, she was seen so many places around the world and did so much good in missionary lands by her appearances that the cloistered nun is now the co-patron of the Missions.

example, "seeing" in imagination cancer cells destroyed by a chemo drug). Nor is it attempting to manipulate God— "claiming" what you pray for, equating this with receiving, say, the claimed physical healing, and judging you lacked faith if what you asked for is not forthcoming. It is, as Solanus taught, letting God be God, surrendering to his will with as much trust as you can muster, or wish you could muster, that God cares for you and divine providence will meet your needs in the way determined best by God. If that is really the case you can afford to thank him even before the needs are met.

3. *Ask and ask again, even to the point that you seem to be pestering, if necessary.*

To do otherwise is to fall into the devilish trap of feeling you show a lack of trust or faith by asking more than once for what you need. The Scriptures tell us to do precisely the opposite, to pester. (Look at what Jesus says in Luke 11:5–13 for one example.)

It certainly is what small children do when they need something and their parents are busy. Saints do it regularly. Consider St. Pio of Pietrelcina, whose impoverished, remote southern Italian town, San Giovanni Rotondo, lost its inadequate hospital in a 1938 earthquake. Padre Pio let God know that a new, larger, altogether more modern hospital was needed and in January 1940 formally started the project requiring millions with a donation of one gold coin given him by a very poor elderly woman. The response of most locals was laughter at Pio's folly.

World War II, fought ferociously on Italian soil with terrible destruction of life and property by massive bombings, left the

South poorer than ever, roadblocking the project. Padre Pio kept after God. One way of doing this was the ongoing novena he recited daily for this and the other prayer burdens he was always carrying for incredible numbers of people.

He kept gently reminding God of God's own words of promise. First he prayed, "O my Jesus, you have said, 'Truly I say to you, ask and it will be given you, seek and you will find, knock and it will be opened to you.' Behold, I knock, and I seek for the grace of . . ." Then he prayed, "O my Jesus, you have said, 'Truly I say to you, if you ask anything of the Father in my name, he will give it to you.' Behold in your name, I ask the Father for the grace of . . .'" Then he prayed, "O my Jesus, you have said, 'Truly I say to you, heaven and earth will pass away, but my words will not pass away.' Encouraged by your infallible words I now ask for the grace of . . ."

Finally after putting God in the corner with Jesus' own words, Pio completed his prayer by reminding Jesus of his love for humankind and for his own mother. His precise words were: "O Sacred Heart of Jesus, for whom it is impossible not to have compassion on the afflicted, have pity on us miserable sinners and grant us the grace which we ask of you, through the Sorrowful and Immaculate Heart of Mary, your tender Mother and ours."

In between each of the first three calls on divine providence, the saint prayed the *Our Father*, the *Hail Mary*, the *Glory Be* and ended with "Sacred Heart of Jesus, *I place all my trust in you.*" He did this on days when the work progressed and on the many days when it came to a standstill for lack of funds. Today the huge hospital towers over the little city.

4. *Put any embarrassment aside and ask others—especially those with more faith than you—to join you in prayer for your needs.*

Asking others to pray for and even with you is one of the smartest things you can do. Their prayer power, their confidence that God will provide, can carry you through the trust-sucking swamp of your doubts and buttress prayers you make with so much less trust and faith than you'd like. It's all part of the "communion" created among believers by the Holy Spirit. If you don't really believe prayer makes any difference, consider it an experiment. If you are one of those who find it extremely hard not to be completely self-sufficient even in your prayer life, and can't bring yourself to ask a person you know, start by calling a prayer line. However you have to ease into it, don't let pride keep you from opening this door into divine providence.

PRAYER IS ALWAYS WORKING

Padre Pio, for instance, enlisted others in the hospital project. When the end of WWII made it possible, he got supporters to set up prayer groups around Italy—there were twenty-three before long—where ordinary people could join in the clamor.[50]

---

50 Naturally, besides praying for the hospital, the groups implored God for Pio's other ministries, as well as praying for the pope, world peace, and each member's own needs.

As Padre Pio and others kept pestering God for the hospital, something very unusual happened: an important English economist and magazine publisher named Barbara Ward (d. 1981) learned of the project and saw the need. Her fiancé, Sir Robert Jackson, was an official at an agency of the United Nations doing postwar reconstruction in Italy. Ward involved Jackson. Jackson involved the United Nations Relief and Rehabilitation Administration (UNRRA).

After sixteen years of prayer by Pio and his friends, in 1956, the large, superbly equipped hospital arose in San Giovanni Rotondo to serve the whole surrounding area—in spite of the fact that its founder, Padre Pio, who was born and would die poor, had no money at any time in his life except what divine providence passed through his hands for this huge project and other good deeds.

A cynic may complain that God didn't act right away or that he involved secular people. Students of mysticism would laugh on both scores. Regarding the divine tardiness, prayer is always working. But God at times first lets it work growing faith and virtue in his petitioners over a long period of persevering prayer. A Protestant clergyman of tremendous faith, George Müller, for instance, once prayed thirty years for another man's conversion before it took place, and it took St. Monica a lifetime of prayers to bring her son St. Augustine to God. In each case the petitioner grew into holiness and the petition was answered in God's "right time." As for employing secular instruments, God regularly uses worldly powers to accomplish divine purposes (for scriptural examples of that, see all the kings, pharaohs, and other leaders God used as instruments in his dealings with the Israelites, whether pouring out blessings upon them or chastising them).

After inaugural talks by notables of church and state, Padre Pio made a short address of thanks. He said, "This is what providence created with your help." I think it fair to say "your help" referred to all those who joined Pio in daily bringing the matter to God's attention for sixteen years—not just those who physically worked on the project or donated money.

Padre Pio is one of many saints who found it smart to enlist prayer armies on their behalf. Mother Teresa of Calcutta, for instance, did this in a big way with affiliated suffering and sick lay members, as well as contemplative branches of her men's and women's communities. In spite of the prayer armies generating so much spiritual fuel, some projects to help humanity still took years, and a few of Mother Teresa's dreams, such as seeing her mother again, never happened in this life. A good reminder to do one's best to follow the saints when, in God's mysterious designs, a prayer is answered "no." For the holy person, that is a reason not for despair or fury or beating oneself up, but to mine deeper into the lode of divine providence.

Follow saints such as Pio and Teresa and practice faith, if you feel the call, by becoming part of some big or little prayer army, maybe a parish, extended family, neighborhood, or group affiliated with a movement or saint that "calls out the troops" when prayer is needed, including for members like you. If you're not a group person, you might join with just one other pray-er. Even two people who partner in prayer can be a powerful force for each other's needs and the needs of others. When praying with a prayer partner or with a group of whatever kind—contemplative, Rosary, charismatic, or ecumenical neighborhood, to mention just some—you may actually *feel* more faith-filled, enabling you to petition divine providence for your needs and those of others with more confidence that God will provide. This isn't "group hysteria" or "the power of suggestion," or any other thing the mind can come up with to explain the spiritual away. It is the presence of God among you.

In some cases another phenomenon jacking up your faith level can be an emission of spiritual energy from the faith or holiness of one or more group members. It reflects the fact that there are people so full of God's love and light that this spills over, affecting and drawing others up spiritually.

A non-Christian friend of mine once experienced this overflow of God's love emanating from Mother Teresa. A concentration camp survivor witnessed this spiritual magnetism in a Hungarian Jewish woman prisoner.[51] St. John Bosco wrote of St. Joseph Cafasso that just running into the older priest revitalized Bosco no matter how exhausted he was. Administering a hospital in an area of Argentina with many poor, Salesian Brother Bl. Artemides Zatti (d. 1951) would reply when anyone complained that using a certain medication on a patient would cost too much, "No, no! Divine providence is rich and will provide everything we need." But a doctor who worked with Zatti testified that more than medicines Zatti was "himself a remedy: he healed people by his presence . . ." A second doctor said, "When I met Brother Zatti, any doubts I had disappeared." If you know anyone who emits this powerful energy and you can pray with them or get them to pray for you, you can benefit enormously.[52]

---

51 Gitta Mallasz, *Talking with Angels* (Daimon Verlag, 1988).

52 If you are in a prayer group with someone like this and find yourself jealous of the person, as I once did, just take it to God. With prayer, healing will come.

Where there is no one of this type in the group you are praying with, your increased faith relates, after God's presence almost certainly, to the add-up factor: your faith plus a companion's faith is stronger than your faith alone and multiplies with more companions. And if you find a prayer companion or group that gives you a temporary faith boost, that lasts at least during the prayer time, you may eventually—especially as you see prayer answers pile up—experience a permanent ascent to a higher level of trust in God's reality and God's loving providence.

5. *Challenge at once any inner suggestions or image of God that suggests it is wrong to petition God for small things that some would dismiss as too trivial for prayer.*

In this sense, be a child with God. After all, doesn't the average parent enjoy hugely providing small delights for a child—whether playing endless peek-a-boo and "I'm going to get you" with the youngest to preparing an older child's favorite food for dinner.

Fifteen-year-old Thérèse Martin entering the Carmel at Lisieux with her boundless confidence in God's love hoped for snow for her January clothing day, even though the weather was mild and springlike. In her autobiography St. Thérèse later wrote:

> [After the ceremony] as I stepped back into the enclosure, the first thing I saw was the statue of the Child Jesus smiling at me . . . Then, turning toward the quadrangle, *I saw it was completely covered with snow!*
> How considerate of Jesus!

Author and spiritual columnist Father Ron Rolheiser wrote of one of his fellow Oblates of Mary Immaculate serving in the far north and traveling by dogsled in winter. On a hot spring evening the priest was using a horse and "a sledlike contraption" to haul supplies from one of his winter way stations, himself afoot. About 9 PM, he met a truck that took the load so the Oblate could ride once more. As he moved slowly along he became dehydrated and began fantasizing about oranges. He went so far as to say a little prayer. And not much farther along there was an orange on the road. Thinking his mind had tumbled from fantasy into full-blown hallucination, he rode on. Then he was inspired by concern for his sanity to go back and dismount. It was a real orange and oh! the sweet delight as he ate it— delight in the fruit and delight in God's tender gesture of love. As he went along his way rejoicing, three more times this joyous experience was repeated. Father Rolheiser, who personally knew his fellow Oblate's sanity and sanctity, explained, "God's providence includes everyday miracles, even miracles of oranges . . ." In other words, nothing in your life is too trivial to interest God if you and the Master of the Universe are on friendly terms!

Such delicate little attentions to needs and desires are commonplace in surrendered lives. Take one more instance of this in the life of a friend of mine, Sharon Burke of Portland, Oregon. Sharon found her washer refusing to work. With five little kids and no money for appliance replacements just then, she told God the washer simply *couldn't* die. It revived with that prayer alone—Sharon says she sensed God chuckle at her frazzled housewife panic—and served the Burkes for seventeen more years!

6. *When you receive what you ask for, don't let any negative part of you assert, "That was just a coincidence!"*

Stop such thoughts immediately, perhaps by saying aloud, "Thanks, God!"

For instance, if you are driving at rush hour on a busy freeway, traffic comes to a standstill, you ask God to let it move, and it does, don't let any inner cynic brush away such little proofs of God's love. Practice instead *dwelling* on such instances with lots of praise and thanksgiving when they occur, and thinking about them afterward. You might even want to tell a faith-filled friend or note it in your gratitude journal if you are keeping one.

Practicing hushing the inner "coincidence!" crier will do wonders for increasing your faith. This is not to encourage you to see a miracle behind every set of intersecting shadows or to insist you received what you asked for if the traffic doesn't move for an hour! The right type of skepticism is very healthy! And the wrong type of "faith" can be pretty silly.

God knows how prone many of us are to doubt, and to brushing away the supernatural through fear. So God over and over again proves to us that a particular blessing is from God and no coincidence by the *precision* of the gift. Remember those instances when Mother Cabrini received the precise amount needed. Here are a few more of these faith-builders.

In terrible economic times of runaway inflation around 1920, St. Maximilian Kolbe got his superior's permission to start a magazine so long as he, not the Franciscans, met all expenses. To do this Max begged door-to-door from people struggling to put bread on the table. The day came when he didn't manage to collect what was needed to pay the printing bill. He went into the church and prayed hard, asking Mary—whom he always called "The Immaculata"—to intercede. He looked up and saw a sack on the altar. Pinned to it was a note: "For my dear mother, Mary Immaculate." Inside was the exact amount owed. Joyously and thankfully, he went to his superior, who let him use the money. Shortly after that a visiting American priest gave Max the funds to buy his own printing press. God provided for the short-term need and provided again for the ongoing one.

CONSIDER GEORGE MÜLLER

As a young fellow, George Müller (d. 1898) was not particularly devout but eventually he surrendered to God. This German landed in Bristol, England, where—now a Protestant clergyman—he pushed to the maximum the scriptural promise "Seek ye first the kingdom of God and his righteousness, and all these things shall be added unto you" (Matthew 6:33). First he stopped taking a regular salary for his preaching. Then he sold all he had and gave what he received to the poor. With his wife's agreement, they gave away their household goods and furnishings.

Yet they got along. Müller then felt led to open an orphanage, that he ran on the following principles: He made the financial needs of the institution known to God, but to no one else. He forbade all his helpers to tell anyone but God as well. He never sought credit or borrowed. He never used money that was donated for anything other than what the giver specified. Thus, if there was no food, but money had been given for coal, for coal it went. It is no exaggeration to claim that the Protestant clergyman spent a lot of time in prayer. Occasionally he was praying right up until the meal the food was needed for. But the meal's provisions always arrived.

George Müller's whole life became a witness to the absolute reliability of divine providence—as were the experiences of the earlier Catholic priest St. Joseph Cottolengo (d. 1842), who ran a hospital and a whole complex of shelters in Turin, Italy, for every type of impoverished unfortunate from the blind, insane, deaf, and crippled to wayward girls. Cottolengo called his whole undertaking simply *The Little House* and, like Müller, looked completely to divine providence to meet the huge and varied needs of such a place. In fact, Cottolengo turned down a subsidy offered by a king because "we are cared for by the King of Kings." Now, if one or two of these two men's needs were met but not all, and if this happened once or even a few times over a long period, it would be reasonable to cite coincidence or luck. But the lives of these two servants of God prove something different. They had huge needs and those needs were indeed met day after day, year after year. Who or what met them? Divine providence.

7. *Give frequent thought to the fact that "due to God's love for me, whether I deserve it or not, God has used divine power on my behalf."*

Perhaps this will scare some of you, particularly if you can't yet see yourself as God's beloved child. For others this type of meditation will be tremendously consoling.

Bl. Mary of Providence (Eugénie Smet; d. 1871) demonstrates the kind of comfortableness with God's goodness and lavish generosity found in many of those who try to be God's friends. She understood how deeply God loves surrendered souls who expect everything like a happy child confidently and joyfully from *le bon Dieu* ("the good God"), as she and other French say.

Having moved some of her first recruits into a house as poor as they, the foundress and superior of the house promptly and symbolically gave the keys to Our Lady of Providence. Then she begged Jesus' Mother to demonstrate her acceptance of being head of the place *and* of their hearts by obtaining from God the following favor: "that on that very day some friend . . . not seen for a long time should come and be inspired to leave an offering. The day wore on," a biographer continues, "but the Blessed Mother was giving no sign of remembering the request." In spite of her enormous confidence, Bl. Mary faltered momentarily at four o'clock. She actually prepared to go out, since it seemed certain no one was coming. As she opened the door, on the stoop, preparing to knock, was an old, wealthy friend not seen for eighteen months. In the joy of friendship renewed, Mary of Providence forgot about her prayer; but before the guest left, she insisted on taking Mary out to buy a gift for the house chapel.

GOD'S LAVISH GENEROSITY

Mary of Providence had her moment of doubt, but after this sign, the foundress reverted to her irrepressible self: "She celebrated this initial favor by arranging an octave (a period of eight days) of welcome to Our Lady, with the further request that every day . . . be marked by some gracious gift or gesture on the part of the new Superior" (i.e., Jesus' mother). Her biographer, insisting "The story of the ensuing days reads like a fairy tale . . . fantastic because it is true," does not give the particulars of every gift of the next eight days, but here are those that are detailed—each arriving without any more maneuvering than that first request. On Sunday a Madame Dumont gave eighty francs to buy vases for the chapel; on Monday when the community was almost out of funds, an unsigned letter arrived containing three hundred francs; Tuesday brought a spiritual gift—the sisters were summoned to a dying woman estranged from God and brought her to a happy death. Next (so probably arriving on the fourth day), beautiful cloth of gold that had belonged to the empress was received, to turn into lovely altar cloths. On the fifth day the Marist Fathers volunteered to say daily Mass for three months in the chapel. Days six and seven are not detailed. On the eighth and final day, Mary of Providence was ill and could not see a visitor who, without giving her name, left eighty francs, while a parish pastor, Abbé Roquette, gave one hundred. There were more favors to the new community that I can't match with a particular day, including a gift of an organ-like instrument called a harmonium.

However frivolous some may see Mary of Providence's prayer request, all these providential gifts served deep spiritual purposes: the period was, in fact, a powerful class in God's grace, letting the new community bask in God's love,[53] unifying the group and gracing each soul. As one of her biographers notes, the gifts created in the Society for all time a trust in divine providence like that of Mary of Providence herself, "who stands forever as an incontrovertible example of the familiar relationship that can exist between earth and heaven, if faith be strong and trust without limitation."

For a relationship with God like that, it is surely worthwhile to keep practicing!

---

53 It was God who bestowed everything, since the Mother of Jesus, like other humans, has no divine power: she prays for those who address needs or desires to her attention. Of course, Jesus chose a mother for himself who is a mighty prayer warrior! Catholics believe no one goes to Mary for help and is left unaided.

CHAPTER Nine

Do Your Part: "Let's Go Dutch" and Other Opportunities to Practice Financial Discipline

W HY, YOU MAY BE ASKING YOURSELF, DO WE NEED A CHAPTER on financial—pardon the dread term—*self-discipline?*

Because even with God, there's no free lunch. While you pray as if everything depends on God, *because it does,* you need to do what you can—remember Solanus slinging those bags of potatoes?—to meet your material and financial needs. Here are some suggestions:

1. *Use your ingenuity or other gifts in meeting your financial needs, as you open yourself to God's providential help.*

A sterling example of this is the future Mother Angelica who felt God's call to leave her monastery in Canton, Ohio to pioneer the Poor Clare Franciscans in Alabama. She had permission from her mother superior and assurance from an Alabama bishop that she and her little group of nuns would be welcome. Still it was necessary to raise money for the new foundation.

Sister Angelica knew God's providence, but she did not turn to prayer alone—although she did plenty of that—and wait for God to provide. The would-be foundress and her spiritual daughters in the Canton community began making and selling fishing lures. They had great success. The money they took in, added to what the Lord provided, took them to Alabama.

In Alabama, to support themselves, the nuns "stuffed envelopes for minimum wage, started a clipping service . . . raised strawberries . . . and more successfully roasted, bagged, and sold peanuts."[54] Around twenty years later Mother Angelica turned from pitching peanuts to pitching the hugely wealthy and various foundations to start a television ministry. Essentially, it was the same principle: pray and trust divine providence, but don't just sit there, do your part.

2. *Even though God loves you, If you willfully live in a way that invites financial disaster, don't expect God to save you from the consequences of your choices.*

Being unwilling to give up the bigger house, fancier car, or more credit-card indulgences than you can actually afford is not the best claim on God's providence. Parents who really love the child who stole the candy bar make sure the kid faces the music with confession to the store manager. In trying to have more than you can honestly earn, you may discover God loves you enough to see you undergo consequences too—perhaps "a severe mercy," a financial collapse such as foreclosure, repossession, or

---

54 Raymond Arroyo, *Mother Angelica: The Remarkable Story of a Nun, Her Nerve, and a Network of Miracles,* (Doubleday, 2005). See pp. 86–89, 90, 93, 97, 109, and 115 on fishing lures, 116, 118, and 124 on peanuts, and 116 on all other efforts at financial self-help.

bankruptcy—so you have the chance to change your disastrous financial style. (Naturally it is possible to have these same financial difficulties for reasons that in no way involve a failure of self-discipline!)

Even should you squeak past financial collapse, in living beyond your means, however devout you are, you'll suffer consequences such as nasty stress that hurts you physically, can make you a cranky parent, spouse, or roommate, and will likely impact negatively the quality of your work and work relationships.

Debt even affects saints. St. John Bosco was personally asked by the pope to build today's Sacred Heart Church in Rome. This gargantuan undertaking meant taking on huge costs that Don (the Italian title for priests) Bosco had to pay for by fundraising that was exhausting because it involved traveling when he was not well. Only because he was a saint did Bosco hold up emotionally and spiritually. On top of his life of self-giving for youth, it was too much physically. As a Salesian biographer put it, "In playing the part of a beggar, he was scattering the remains of his health on the road." A doctor had already told Bosco his body was so worn out, it was no longer good for anything but "to hang up in the closet." The church was consecrated in May 1887. Don Bosco died the next January. A good reminder to you and me that debt, even for good causes, is truly a heavy burden on body, mind, and soul.

3. *Follow a simple life plan.*

Studying married saints or single lay saints is to see time and again money used in spiritually healthy ways. For example, successful business owners Bl. Louis and Bl. Zélie Martin kept their lives uncomplicated. With no desire to measure themselves against others financially (or in any other way), they lived comfortably but with no effort to keep up with other families. In fact, the Martins avoided mixing with the wealthy and well connected as much as they could, convinced that the exaggerated valuation of money, status, and social position espoused by most of these people might lead their children down false roads to an illusory happiness. This does not mean they lived in bizarre asceticism. Photos show they and their five daughters very nicely dressed—the children even more than the parents. Zélie did delight in turning out her girls! And their home and furnishings were equally appropriate for their situation: handsome without being ostentatious.

Ven. Pierre Toussaint (d. 1853), who was imported as a slave from Haiti, became a successful New York hairdresser to the city's elite. He and eventually his wife also lived simply without affectations either of success or pious poverty. With heroic charity, he supported the elderly, penniless "owner" who had offered him his freedom. Pierre's simple lifestyle gave him the satisfaction of helping many other needy people, including youngsters seeking education. He and his wife—whose freedom he had bought—also took on raising his dead sister's child.

Today it is harder to live in dignified simplicity like the Martins or Toussaint, and dozens of other saints did, because of the change in the American, and world, economy. Our nation's wealth came originally from production by farming, manufacturing, crafts making, and services that met real needs. Now, in a spiritually sick situation, it comes from "consuming."

Desire is created or amplified via the manipulation of minds and hearts. This leads to a great deal of buying on credit, creating debt plus interest plus fees. Living by this system you never have "enough": as soon as you have "A" (and likely owe for it), created desire convinces you that you must have "B" as well. Consumerism, with its message that it's natural to pay for everything by "charging" or borrowing, might as well be called "debt-ism."

If you are rich like the Drexel family, who could do good, have the best of everything, and still be awash in money, skip this part. For the rest, here is a way, *obviously just a suggestion*, you could choose to manage your financial life to achieve the dignified simplicity of the saints.

Opt out of consumerism and debt. For the health of your mind, soul, and body—this will take prayer for many—live *under* your income. Moreover, without being slavish about it, give 10 percent to God, donating that as God inspires (certainly give some to the place where you worship, which has bills like you). Save 10 percent in a federally insured account. Live on the rest. If you can't afford a house, get an apartment. If, just out of school, you can't afford an apartment, rent a room. Pay debt off before incurring more. And incur debt only for major things such as a home.

If you use a credit card, buy nothing you can't pay for that month, so you never pay any interest (if that's beyond you, freeze the card in a huge block of ice so you have it for building credit but can't use it without time for thought). Living this way, if you are in debt, will slowly get you out of debt. If you are not in debt, barring catastrophes, this will keep you out. If you have a health catastrophe, use a religiously based or other hospital where they will set up a repayment plan you can afford. As for investing, keep it safe, simple, and secondary to your savings plan. One last suggestion: don't be sucked into false economy. To give just one example: skipping fresh produce and eating cheap, fatty meats are two ways to save money immediately that are apt to prove costly down the road in medical-dental expenses, to say nothing of bodily misery. If the thought of a higher weekly grocery bill makes you squirm, know that a number of people have successfully cancelled out the cost of the healthy food by cutting back on unhealthy items.

MERCY BEYOND TELLING

Be sure that if you want to live simply, God will help you. Be sure, too, that all this financial self-discipline does not mean living meanly and miserably, or tediously recording every penny spent. Instead it permits you to get much more out of whatever money you have for yourself and others. The difference, for instance, in saving first, then paying cash for cars—*used* is not a dirty word by the way—and appliances or buying on credit and paying interest is often enough to buy another big-ticket item. Above all, use self-discipline in your finances to *enjoy* a life free of *self-created* monetary stresses.

Moreover this lifestyle—practiced by Bl. John XXIII for one, who wanted to die poor but said he would mind greatly dying in debt[55]—has many bonuses for those who like to help others: your thermos and brown bag model simplicity, as opposed to arriving at work, expensive latte in hand, and heading midday for a restaurant lunch (assuming you can't afford either). So does saying openly to a similarly paid colleague, "Let's go Dutch," instead of jockeying to see who gets stuck with the full bill neither can afford. By such honesty, you can help create or sustain a fashion for living simply and within your means. And by doing your part, you position yourself wonderfully for God's bounty.

Having said that refusing to curb your material appetites is not the best claim on God's providence, let me give God's mercy-beyond-telling its due. St. Gabriel Possenti (d. 1862), who had had his share of the good life before becoming a Passionist priest, was sent by God a couple of years after his early death at age twenty-four to his younger brother Vincent. Barely into his twenties Vincent's morally dubious lifestyle had already gotten him into terrible debt. Gabriel gave him a talking to on behalf of God. Then, like the manna that once dropped from heaven, God's messenger left behind a way to clear the debt. For your fresh start, I wouldn't count on something supernatural (and certainly don't try to contact the dead: when God wants such meetings, God arranges them). But don't rule God's mercy out either, *however it manifests itself* when there is real sorrow for one's financial idiocies (or idiocies of any kind) and real desire to change.

---

55 He borrowed to help his peasant-sharecropper father own his own farm and, that paid off, many years later borrowed to help a brother do the same. He never tried to own a residence for himself, but he used cash in hand to improve places he lived at various postings that were owned by the Catholic Church.

4. Rather than just continuing your spending habits as usual and hoping for the best in a time of need, seek bargains.

Mother Cabrini received amazing divine assistance when she was up against various financial walls. But those who did business with her knew she was a serious businessperson when it came to financial outlays and commitments. She knew how to bargain with suppliers where appropriate, and how to furnish her hospitals, orphanages, and schools at the lowest possible cost by searching out used, remaindered, discounted, or giveaway bargains. In short, the saint practiced careful stewardship, even as, paradoxically, she relied totally on divine providence. If you are afraid, as one relative told me, that if you don't shop at the best places, you won't get quality merchandise, take a stroll through a discount store with your eyes open. You could be surprised.

5. You may be helped by having a budget or financial plan of some sort to free you from misguided use of money.

When Padre Pio was building that huge hospital that today sits across from the friary where he lived, he had the designers and builders keep a budget. Then he had a financial plan stunning in its simplicity. He simply refused to apply for loans or take on debt: when the money wasn't there, the work halted until divine providence provided more funds. I know two couples who built homes the same low-stress way.

On the other hand, it must be admitted that if you truly partner with God, it is possible to operate even large enterprises without a budget. Catholic broadcaster Mother Angelica told Father John Catoir that at a time when she needed $200,000 each month to broadcast the EWTN signal and meet other expenses, sometimes she began the month with $600. "We trust in God's providence," she explained, adding she loved to confound business "big shots" who asked, "Do you have a budget?" by replying, "I don't believe in budgets."

The mischievous nun told Catoir, as she did *not* tell the poor frustrated businessmen, that people in business *should* have a budget, but she was not in business. "I'm doing the Lord's business," she spells out. So, when a businessman advised her to come up with a figure, say $100,000, for a year's costs and then raise that amount, she replied playfully, "But what if God wanted to give me $400,000? I just lost $300,000 and that would break my heart."

Yes, not everyone needs a financial plan. A Mother Angelica can do just fine without one. However, it was she who, in my own hearing, told the following: asked why, if she was a woman of such great faith, she took so much upset-stomach medication, she replied, "I *am* a woman of great faith; my stomach just doesn't know that." Stress!

6. *To do your part, learn the difference between generosity that is prudent and "generosity" that is unwise or even wrong.*

This is an area where many good people get confused. For example, responding to every charity, church, or human appeal (such as a friend or relative who asks for a loan) when you can't pay all your own present and upcoming expenses, especially if you have others to support, does not ensure that God "owes" you. It can just be a lack of sense. Saying no, far from making you look bad or ruining your relationships, may have surprisingly beneficial outcomes.

Swiss mystic Adrienne von Speyr (d. 1967), whose goal was to become a physician, received a lot of financial support from her extended family after her father's death during her secondary school years and her time in a TB sanatorium. But when it came to medical school, believing she couldn't do it physically, her physician uncle said for that reason he could not give her any financial help. Adrienne worked her way through, learning many useful lessons, receiving help from divine providence, and ending up closer to her beloved uncle. His saying no had expressed the true love that wants the best for the other regardless of how that may have to make you look.

I once had to say no to a request for a loan from someone with whom the relationship was a bit rocky, even though financial gifts had been given in the past. To my stupefaction, the person, learning I was in no position to help, feeling we were in similar straits, became very warm and friendly, as in the times before I had made the well-meant gifts. Saying no, far from ruining a relationship, revitalized it.

Sometimes generosity can even be wrong. For instance, it's no virtue to buy the office gang lunch if you can't pay off the credit card on which you charged it at the end of the month, or if the cash you used was meant to pay the utility bill. Such "generosity" may be abuse of one's dependents. Also, it's no virtue to make others believe they will look bad unless they spend what they can't afford to emulate you.

A final thought: if you have savings or a good income, it's not being loving, kind, and generous to give from them so lavishly that you pay no attention to your future retirement costs. To end up being an unnecessary financial burden to your family *even if it was they to whom you gave so generously* will not just be hard on you, it will be hard on them. And gratitude for your earlier gifts may be replaced by resentment, and perhaps even a surly inquiry why you didn't use some common sense to provide ahead for yourself.

7. *If your sense of self-worth depends on giving, while you pray for healing, take defensive action.*

Try finding a trusted spiritually and financially mature person who will let you occasionally run by them donations, gifts, and even loans you desire or feel pressured to make. Seeking guidance is especially advisable if an inner voice warns you can't really afford to do what you are contemplating. A second defensive action is to roadblock your impetuosity ahead of time. Actually think about your overall giving in terms of what you can afford to give, so that, when suddenly asked for a donation, loan, or gift, you aren't completely at the mercy of your desire to look good, perceive yourself as generous, be loved, or whatever.

If you tend to go all mushy when relatives you love seek a loan or gift, and give beyond what you can afford or in situations where saying yes may actually be harmful to the seeker, all because you don't know how to say no, pray and practice ways suited to your temperament to get out this short, wonderful word.

Be heartened by Servant of God Père Jacques Bunel, the French Carmelite educator caught sheltering Jewish youths, who gave his life for others as a concentration camp prisoner. There is a moving testimony about Père Jacques by a student the headmaster expelled. Looking back as an adult, the witness explains that when Père Jacques informed him in the headmaster's office that he was being expelled, it was done with such fatherliness, such genuine love and concern for the boy, that that disciplinary meeting changed his life. He also says that Père Jacques was right in the sense of being justified by the boy's behavior to say no to his remaining a pupil of the school. But beyond justice, severing the boy from the institution was part of the good the priest did him. Imagine! Finding the courage to say a loving, firm no may make you part of God's loving providence.

Perhaps your weakness is greatest when face-to-face with a donation-seeker at your door. To save yourself from yourself, decide on and even practice what you are going to say. One charming relative of mine says pleasantly that she and her husband are retirees on a fixed income and can't give. If pressed further, she smiles, laughingly says, "Go away," and gently shuts the door. Another person handles the temptation by a commitment to herself to tell the solicitor in kind tones, "I have my charities" (no specifying to avoid attempts to change those) "and can't take on new ones, so I don't give to any door-to-door appeals." It works because it is said with conviction. She does the same with phone solicitations.

If you have to give something to solicitors, you can give something nonmonetary but valuable. Praise the person going door-to-door for donating their time to their cause. You can even tell a solicitor, whose cause you can say (pleasantly!) you don't support, that this is what makes democracy work. This respect for each person as a child of God whose opinions may change—perhaps triggered to re-examine an issue just because someone "on the other side" was kind, not the monster they expected—was the style of Bl. John XXIII.

The holidays, when anxiety to show your love is highest, can be the toughest time of all. If the season typically ends with you in debt, pray hard to understand love. Then well ahead of time set your limits. Maybe a dollar amount, maybe your need to draw names this year rather than giving to each person.

NON-MATERIAL GIFTS

Maybe declaring that all your gifts will be homemade, such as food you cook or preserve, flowers you dry, or an item you sew. Or, if you really haven't or shouldn't spend any money at all, announce you are giving "tickets" for such things as a hike together, babysitting, repotting houseplants, half a day of filing, weeding, etc. Wouldn't you yourself love some of these? Whatever you do, do it warmly! If tempted to falter, remind yourself that the example you are setting is itself a huge gift.

Perhaps in doing your part in meeting your financial/material needs, you can't always buy a child gifts they want. Where parents and grandparents are unselfish and loving, family hard times are a teaching opportunity about not buying what can't be afforded and about real riches. Caring trumps all. With or without material means, you can if desired find something to give, because love finds a way to express itself "and is a gift no money can buy."

CHAPTER *Ten*

Don't Block the Flow

Evelyn Maxson of Eagle Rock, California, was a vibrant woman who never married, loved to gather and sell to benefit her favorite charity, and always had a soft spot in her heart for those who did not fall into the category one calls "poor" but were young, starting-out couples or "nice" families with economic challenges.

When thanked for her gracious gifts or for selling something of her own at a ridiculously low price, the Episcopalian-bred Unity member would smile and say the more she sent out, the more came in. The "more" was not big checks or stock dividends—she was not well-off and relied personally on divine providence—but boxes of things, many very nice, that people gave her, knowing if she didn't need them herself, she'd "find a home" for that TV or set of dishes at one of the charity sales where she volunteered or as part of her personal outreach. As Evelyn always insisted, the secret to that constant supply from divine providence was, "Don't block the flow."

In fact, this principle of divine providence is universally true. While it is a fact that God wants you to practice financial prudence and to care for dependents and yourself with some worldly wisdom ("Be wise as a serpent" [Matthew 10:16] is just one Scripture that could be cited), it is important not to block the flow of God's supply.

Fortunately, *God will never leave anyone surrendered to providence with nothing to give.* Don't worry if it's little: while even saints may not appear to have much to give, in providence something little can have big results.

CONSIDER JOHN BOSCO

Joseph Brosio, one of St. John Bosco's closest helpers for forty-six years, one day overheard a visitor's conversation with the saint. Begging for help, the stranger told Don Bosco that his five children were fainting with hunger. Joseph Brosio smelled a con. He watched with disapproval as Don Bosco, nearly penniless himself, rummaged around until he found a few coins and gave the man the tiny amount of money with words of compassion and his priestly blessing.

Afterward the saint told Brosio he wished he had been able to give more, even a large sum, because of the man's need. Believing he'd just witnessed some sob-spinner take advantage of Don Bosco's celebrated compassion, Bosco's helper bluntly suggested the visitor was a con man.

Bosco countered that the man was (in Brosio's later written testimony[56]) "sincere and honest . . . a hard worker and very

---

56 *Biographical Memoirs of St. John Bosco*, Vol. 3, 348–49.

devoted to his family." Like financially secure families in every era, it was just "misfortune," claimed Bosco, that had plunged this family into abject poverty. Unconvinced, Joseph Brosio insisted. How did Don Bosco *know* all that was actually the case? Don Bosco confided he knew by divine illumination or, as the saint put it, "I read his heart."

However you are inclined to take that, consider this: sometime later Brosio ran into the begging visitor. Far from fleeing like a typical con artist, he was eager to talk. From him Joseph Brosio got an unforgettable glimpse into the breadth and depths of divine providence, where, given compassionately by one of God's friends out of that person's own need, "a little bit" becomes more than enough.

The few coins Don Bosco had been able to give him, the man told Brosio, were barely enough to buy a little bit of corn flour, an amount that would make about two servings of polenta (corn porridge). The man continued, "We now speak of him [Bosco] as the priest who wrought the 'miracle of the polenta' because seven of us (the five children and parents, each desperately hungry) were able to eat our fill." In addition, the man told Brosio that, after the saint's blessing, the family's luck had completely turned. Since taking his sad story to the saint, "his affairs had improved day by day."

Not only can we always give—even if only a prayer—it is vital to our emotional and spiritual well-being that we do give. Don Bosco, for instance, with a building full of boys and young men dependent upon him for their daily bread, their schooling, their very clothing (simple suits that for years he cut out and sewed himself), would have been faulted by no one had he sympathized with his caller but told the man he had no money to give him. But Bosco, who said many times he relied absolutely on divine providence, knew from countless instances not to block the flow.

He was indeed God's providence for a needy family. God was there time and again for Don Bosco in his needs, too. This was not, however, always immediately obvious. God led this saint by a completely different road than a Mother Teresa. He was forever running lotteries or appealing to his wealthy benefactors or the government for funding. Often he would be at zero financially—this burden, too, part of his heroically sacrificial life for the young. Such was the case one morning when, hearing confessions, he was interrupted by the doleful whisper that there weren't enough rolls in the house for the boys' breakfast and the baker would give no more credit. Bosco whispered back to gather up whatever buns could be found, and he'd come hand them out himself, then he turned back to the more important task of helping a soul.

A youth named Francis Dalmazzo, who hadn't been happy at the establishment because of the quality and quantity of the food, overheard this exchange. His mother was picking him up, and he had come for a last confession with Don Bosco. When she arrived he asked her to wait a few minutes. He went over to watch Don Bosco give out the buns—Francis counted fifteen— to the group of some four hundred boys. Positioning himself just above and behind where he could see the priest's every move, Francis Dalmazzo watched Don Bosco give each boy a smile, a kind word, and a bun. When the last boy had taken his roll, Francis counted: there were still fifteen rolls. And since their father in God said nothing, the only one to notice the amazing action of divine providence was the boy who planned to leave.

Make that *had* planned to leave. Having just seen divine providence multiply mite into miracle, Francis told his mother he was sorry to have written her and brought her all the way to get him. He had changed his mind. He stayed to become one of Bosco's Salesians and left his testimony of one of the multiplications in the life of Bosco—and others like him who know how not to block the flow.

Some reader about now is muttering that in the previous chapter, giving when you can't afford it is said to be wrong. Now, giving from your very lack is held up as a wonderful thing that keeps divine providence flowing and even produces miracles.

A bit of differentiation will help. I know well a young woman who some years back received a phone call from the illegitimate son of one of her very respectable uncles. Jared was in town and was broke, but he had a chance for a job, if he could purchase the necessary protective clothing. The young woman, an orphan who was her own sole support and also helped her grandmother monthly, promptly gave him half the money in her one bank account—half what she had in the world.

Was this foolish? Not really. She had a nine-month teaching contract, that she knew would more than cover her monthly expenses for months to come. She owed no one anything. Her inexpensive secondhand car had been bought with cash. She had no house to provide insurance, mortgage payments, and maintenance for. She had no spouse or children. And she had recently become a Catholic, wanted to live the gospel, and had a small hope her gift might witness to Jared, whom she cared about.

My young woman friend's case is quite different from the man I thought of as I wrote in the previous chapter that taking the office gang to lunch may be abusive of one's family. This charming gentleman had emotional-spiritual issues that caused him to pick up the tab repeatedly while his children and wife lacked basic necessities. The debts he ran up—in the claws of his obsession to be seen as generous—eventually caused his good and responsible wife, who had no religious background that might deter her, to divorce him for a saner, debt-free existence. Inappropriate "generosity" became a tragedy for this family.

St. John Bosco was called as a priest mentor and example to several thousand young men to live on a heroically high spiritual level. For him to give out of his want was an appropriate part of his particular call to sanctity. It was, the saint believed, as did his spiritual children in the next generation, a guarantee that God would provide.

Bl. Michael Rua (d. 1910), whom Bosco mentored from an early age, became a Salesian and succeeded Bosco as head of the Salesian order. At one point Don Rua wrote a confrere in South America, "The [Salesian] Houses in France are in great distress, and I find myself embarrassed [not] to [be able to] meet their most urgent requests." At the same time, Rua got a letter from a Salesian in Rome, where funds had suddenly become available to continue a project that had stopped due to lack of money. Would Don Rua okay beginning the work again? Rua answered yes, go ahead with the project, but "only on one condition, namely, that . . . [this group of Salesians] accept at least fifty poor"—meaning young men seeking the vocational training that would change their lives, but unable to pay full freight for themselves. "Then," he concluded, "divine providence will never fail us." With this sort of attitude, whatever their debts and financial worries and burdens, the Salesians kept the flow going and became, as they remain today, the second largest order in the Catholic Church, and a source of providence for the many thousands of needy youth they educate holistically—mind, soul, and body—in schools, workshops, and play centers.

THE RICH BENEFIT TOO

The rich also benefit from not blocking the flow.

I have mentioned the parents of St. Katharine Drexel, who were extremely good, philanthropic, devout people in spite of living with the temptations of great wealth and of belonging to America's nineteenth-century social elite. Emma Bouvier Drexel opened her doors regularly to receive all comers who needed financial help in the pre-welfare era. A woman as shrewd as she was kind, she verified her clients' needs. For needs that proved real, Mrs. Drexel provided rent and food money and also arranged for an abandoned or widowed woman's children to receive training and/or employment when they reached the right age. This direct charity did much more good than if Emma Drexel had subsidized an office and manager somewhere. Her personal, public giving set the whole of Philadelphia society a tremendous example, and enabled her to draw her daughters into the work for each one's spiritual and psychological growth as they came of appropriate age.

Mr. Drexel, busy in his world of banking and high finance, made gifts of money to causes he judged worthy. Publicizing those requests would have been counterproductive, leading, no doubt, to appeals from places he felt no call to help.

The benefits to the Drexels can only be sketched broadly. Financially, the money kept pouring in. The Drexel family was among the richest in America. The family lifestyle of surrender and service to God, including passing on a goodly share of the wealth God gave them (scripturally and traditionally this is a 10 percent tithe of earnings[57]), rooted the couple and their three daughters in a spiritual and emotional stability that led all five to happy, productive lives, not always usual for their social class.

If you have no money to give, don't worry. Non-material things may also keep the flow of divine providence going. Mother Teresa of Calcutta repeatedly urged people to give the valuable gifts of a smile, a word of cheer, or a bit of time to listen. And we don't need to go to the end of the world or even the end of the block to make these gifts of human kindness. Mother Teresa urged people to look for those in their own families suffering isolation, loneliness, and love-deprivation. Pray if family hurts make that hard; and, if necessary, trade families with a friend in this sort of giving, since sometimes the last person one can open

---

57 Whether the amount given by the Drexels was more or less, archivist Dr. Stephanie Morris of St. Katharine's shrine in Bensalem, Pennsylvania, couldn't pin down. Dr. Morris writes, "I suspect that like his daughters, Francis Drexel did things quietly and without fanfare; we may never know the full amount of his charitable donations." Then she adds there is one hint in his will that Francis tithed: at his death, 10 percent of his worth was immediately distributed to charities.

up to, sadly, is a loved one and, even sadder, sometimes the last person you can give to is one of your own.

A simple helping hand is a wonderful gift that facilitates flow. I have never forgotten the frail woman I met in a supermarket decades ago. Alone in the world, her daughter dead at her nursing school in a tragic accident, and her other child, a son, and his wife having cut her off, she wasn't sitting around pickling in the brine of self-pity. On a cold December day she was shopping for a neighbor even frailer than herself and, having no car, was carrying the grocery bag on foot. What a lesson she taught me about always having something to give, even as divine providence sent me to drive her home.[58]

Give respect to others in order to open the flow of divine providence for them and you. The need to treat each other well is recognized by all major faith traditions. Pope John XXIII's long years as a Catholic church diplomat living and working with people of every kind grew his commitment to demonstrate *respect* for everyone. A person's or a movement's beliefs might be askew and one could lovingly challenge those beliefs, but the *person* was created and loved by God. If John as pope had to have a book's theological errors proclaimed, he insisted on a clear distinction between views and their holder so the author would not be condemned as a person. It was this attitude, even more than John's warmth and good humor, that made him the first pope to be widely loved world over by people with no Catholic connection.

Father Emile Brière has written that Catherine de Hueck Doherty, during the Great Depression of the 1930s, referred

---

58 See an account of this incident in *Word Among Us*, February 2009.

to as "Christophers" (Christ-bearers) the men whom others, less respectfully, termed "bums." When a Christopher entered her Toronto House of Hospitality, Catherine made the man welcome "in a most expansive way, leading him personally to a humble bench at a humble table . . . as if she were the gracious hostess of the wealthiest establishment." This outpouring of love and "warm graciousness" gave broken men back their dignity.[59]

Treating others—from intellectuals to the down-and-out—with the respect demonstrated by John and Catherine opens doors in sometimes amazing ways. In college out of a genuine interest in and respect for other cultures, I was friendly to foreign students. One Southeast Asian invited me to a home-cooked meal of his country's foods. To my surprise the dean of my college department was another guest and drove me home. In conversation I mentioned that for financial reasons I was going to transfer to my home state for my senior year. I was open with him that I wanted to spend some time in Europe and, my parents now both being dead, the change to in-state tuition was a way I could do that. Shortly after, I received a merit scholarship I had not even applied for that made up the out-of-state tuition costs!

An attitude of respect for others—whether it ever pays your tuition or not—will open doors to better deals when you are a buyer, and to advancement in the many jobs where the ability to deal well with people of all varieties is a looked-for skill.

Nothing is more important to keep providence gushing than forgiveness, a gift hugely beneficial not just to the recipient but even more to the giver and society. We've seen examples of that already,

---

59 Emile Brière, *Katia* (Les Éditions Paulines, 1988) 71–72.

but because it is so crucial to positioning yourself to reap the
maximum from divine providence, here are two more.

FORGIVENESS OPENED A DOOR (TO BLESSINGS)

A nineteen-year-old student of metallurgic engineering, Paul
Caporali had been surrendered to Christ since he fell "in love
with him" somewhere around the age of sixteen or seventeen.
Paul was home in his native Terni with his mother, his fiancée, Lea, and his sister and her toddler on August 11, 1943,
when American planes bombed the Italian city during WWII.
Although Paul survived, and his father and two younger brothers were later found alive, after the bombing the young student
found those he loved the most were dead. They had headed
toward a shelter a few minutes too late. As he knelt at the grisly
site, Paul wrote in his 2009 memoir, "I wanted to curse the bombers, but a deep surging of Christian pity arose . . . and looking
up at the sky I called out, 'Father, forgive them! They know not
what they do!' And I meant it. *They're soldiers*, I thought, bowing
my head: *They are only carrying out commands.*"

Experiencing "desolation too strong for tears," Paul found in
his fiancée's purse a little prayer book he himself had given her.
He read the words Lea would have meditated on that morning
after her daily Mass: "Do not be overly distressed if I take
something from you; it is mine [and] I take it back."

"Thanks a lot, Lord," he said with momentary bitterness.
Continuing reading, he came to the words, "If I take something
good from you, it is to give you something better." Lea had told

Paul that if the devout youth ever felt a call to the priesthood she would work to put him through the seminary. "Trying to get rid of me?" he had teased this selfless woman—who, like him, put God above everything. Immediately with her death he knew marriage could no longer be in his future. Lea could never be replaced.

Some years after his harrowing loss, the ways of providence led Paul Caporali to become a Salesian priest sent to work in the very country whose bombers had killed those he loved. Because of that earlier, wholehearted forgiveness, the Italian priest has been able to help countless *American* souls forgive their own tragedies, opening them to all the joys of living in the flow of divine providence.[60]

Then there was St. Mary MacKillop (d. 1907) of Australia, a Scot and a capable woman in a sea of Irish clergy in the late nineteenth century. To them—no matter how capable she might be—a woman's only right was to follow men's orders. Mary should have been emotionally and spiritually destroyed by life under such a stricture and, indeed, by the attitudes and behavior of the majority of the men in her life. She passed from support-ing the entire family, due to the instability of her father, into control by an unstable priest, nominal founder of the order she started to bring the faith and education to poverty-stricken chil-dren in remote areas. When the unstable priest exiled her from his presence, she came under an iron-fisted, anti-female bishop

---

60 Father Paul's story of divine providence through his close relationship with the mother of Jesus is privately published as *And Now You Will Be My Mom! (A Marian Story)*.

who set out to crush this uppity nun who claimed, truthfully, that Rome, not he, had control of the fledgling order of Sisters.

Most piteous was the other bishop—well disposed but mentally and physically failing—into whose befuddled ears came whispers from more clergymen determined to destroy her that Mother MacKillop was a secret drinker. He expelled and dismissed her from her order for a time. With God's grace as well as the gift of a brother who had become a Jesuit, to whom she could vent her feelings, Mary forgave them all, even as she stood up for herself and her work. She called some of her non-school foundations housing the needy The Providence in honor of God, who clearly let them open and kept them afloat in such a sea of hostility. But it was forgiveness that cleared her heart and hands to let divine providence pass through them tremendous benefits for huge numbers of children, the women who joined her—and herself.

Perhaps you've been making sincere efforts to follow the principles for living in divine providence. Particularly, you've been doing what you can for yourself through financial discipline. Even if you're not living for God to the degree of a Mary MacKillop—how many of us are!—you're still positioned Godward.

Don't let comparing yourself to any saint or other feelings of inadequacy stop you, if you are feeling ready to see if this principle actually works. Many years back, only partially surrendered to God, I gave "getting into the flow of providence" a whirl when needs brought tears of frustration. Eeking out a small charitable gift, I immediately received a notice of mortgage-payment reduction.

Happily, this is one case where you don't have to think big! Remember Chiara Lubich and friends giving away five eggs (someone brought them a dozen) or an apple (a case arrived). Give prayerfully whatever you can spare—eggs, an apple, a dollar or two, or maybe a sandwich. The result will boost your faith.

GIVING TO BLESS, NOT TO BE SEEN

As you get into this lifestyle, to let providence flow maximally, do your best to avoid two things: giving for display and phony giving. Regarding giving for display, ask God's help not to be the image-driven person of whom it can be said, "Not one of So-and-so's good deeds goes unpublicized." Giving secretly is satisfying, Scripture-recommended—and elicits divine recompense. Of course, you may have a position where you serve by your public example or need to model giving for your children. Moguls Warren Buffett and Bill and Melinda Gates exemplify both, as Emma Drexel did in her day. Some in that position have the humility to give publicly without ego inflation and to combine major public gifts with hidden ones as well. Certainly the three living people just mentioned show no signs of out-of-control egos to this date. You can get a picture of healthily blending the public and private from Servant of God Terence Cardinal Cooke (d. 1983). In his role as Cardinal of New York, Cooke was called to take part in many public good works, both Catholic and civic, lending his prestige and presence to benefits raising money for many important institutions and projects to benefit the human family. He did that graciously but kept secret the work he did one-on-one with AIDS patients, the lepers of his day. That secret charity was atop another secret: that he himself for years was sick with leukemia. The hidden self-giving kept this holy man in a balance that the public, ego-stroking accolades for his visible good deeds might potentially have upset.

However, if you are involved in some visible charitable organization or work, such as a food bank or community kitchen, and you find yourself at times battling pride or self-righteousness, be heartened that this goes with the territory. Dorothy Day speaks extensively on these struggles in her own life with her interviewer Robert Coles in *Dorothy Day: A Radical Devotion.*[61] Awareness of them is actually a sign of spiritual growth. If you can be honest with yourself, as Dorothy was, about your ego's maneuverings, you will grow way beyond those who maintain a persona that masks such human weakness and find yourself closer to God, as well.

MAKING A GIFT GENUINE

Second, avoid phony giving where you hand over to the poor, say, something you want to be rid of as if it were a real gift. Yet in God's tender mercy, I can testify that I once gave away food because a priest asked me to do so to a young inner-city family dealing with the father's catastrophic illness. Most of that food I was glad to get rid of, and I was definitely willing to

---

61 Da Capo Press, Radcliffe Biography Series, see particularly pp. 113–20.

look good, yet I still came home to some very nice cuts of meat brought over by a neighbor who was moving away. Maybe some of us practicing not blocking the flow have to discover God exists and cares about us by receiving divine providence when we are definitely not worthy of it.

CHAPTER *Eleven*

Pass It On!

> If my heart is one with the will of God,
> it will see thousands of other hearts
> coming to life around it.
> —Words of an eleventh-century Buddhist monk

WHEN YOU HAVE PRACTICED THESE TENETS FOR POSITIONING yourself to receive from God's boundless supply long enough, you will know down to your bone marrow—even when economic storms seem to belie it and even if your disposition will always be prone to anxiety and/or doubt—that God will provide.

When suffering hits hard you'll *know* the answer is to go deeper in God. And when you reach the deepest you can go at that time and find—instead of the joy some saints know underneath all circumstances—only apparent emptiness, you'll trust the mystery.

At this stage, you will be living more and more in the freedom of the children of God, refusing ever more readily to take up "God space" with hatreds, grudges, jealousy or envies, greed or stinginess, and all the other miseries you might formerly have clung to. Oh, there will be moments when you will—or at least be tempted to—either rebel against some trial or blame God for the obstacles in the path you are on. You'll be in good company. Teresa of Avila (d. 1582), traveling for God and falling face down in the mud, snorted, "If this is the way you treat your friends, it's no wonder you have so few."

And you can be sure there will still be obstacles. (Saints such as Teresa, in spite of her momentary anger, sometimes actually welcome these at a certain high point in the spiritual ascent where they are equipped to benefit from what can cause harm lower on the spiritual ladder.)[62] But when you falter momentarily under some new burden in believing that all things—even those God merely permits rather than desires—will work for your good in the end, you will be called back by the loving Spirit to nestle again in the sheltering arms of providence.

Looking around you, even in your hardest times, you will see how blessed you are. Not all your wants but all your needs, as God sees them, sooner or later will be met.

Moreover your whole understanding about financial-material realities will have shifted. The financial will be important, but you will know there is more even to the material side of life. Whether getting and spending, buying and selling, building the new enterprise or keeping life in some long-established one—all your economic activity will be lived more and more in creative (junior) partnership with God. Surprising doors will open, for which you can only, shaking your head in wonderment, pour out praise and thanksgiving.

In fact, you will not only thank God untiringly for his many blessings; your increasing love for the Giver and consequent

---

62 She said that while she shrank from suffering (like any sensible person), at times she saw so much good come out of it for her soul that she had to desire trials for those wonderful fruits.

compassion for all God's other children will make you long to pass on what you have learned. Here are just a few of the myriad ways saints have shared the wonderful news of divine providence—passing it on!

A LIFE CAN SPEAK LOUDER THAN WORDS

In the case of St. Maximilian Kolbe, his whole life shines. Intellectually brilliant but very humble, Kolbe was a communications genius who became a Conventual Franciscan. Photographs of friars operating modern communications machinery in his publications drew eight hundred young men to his side in Poland before the war to create the largest friary in the world. They stayed because Kolbe was a joyous, holy man for others. He had no financial resources for this huge place—from which the gospel was being preached in every known media—but he had learned, as he told Brother Jerome Wierzba, "The cashbox of divine providence has no bottom." Particularly his last months strikingly reveal the heights that trust in divine providence can reach.

In dread Auschwitz, where terror made nervous wrecks of even the strong, Kolbe astounded other prisoners by a demeanor that revealed his complete sense of security. He explained to another prisoner why he had no fear in a hell where all were terrified: he saw himself *provided for*, with one hand in Jesus' and one hand in Mary's.

Moreover, in this world of skeletal inmates, the Franciscan was unafraid to pass on some of his starvation-level rations to others. Kolbe lived on in spite of a calorie intake that should have killed him.[63] Where death stalked all, his life was not taken until he awed the Nazi commander by volunteering to die for another man, passing on, a survivor later testified, "a mighty explosion of [life-giving] light."

SOLITARY PRAYER BY A FRIEND OF GOD

Prayer all by itself, in those living a deep spiritual life, can pass on divine providence. Parisian Elizabeth Leseur (d. 1914)[64] stands for millions whose profound living of divine providence passes basically unnoticed outside—and sometimes even within—a small life circle. Certainly it was unrecognized by her husband, Felix, who was determined to save his charming, intelligent wife from the superstition of belief in God.

Elizabeth never argued with him. As much as her health permitted, she lived a full social and happy marital life. But in an environment hostile to God, let alone God's providence—their friends were materialists and often atheists—by living love, Elizabeth attracted people by the inner light she radiated.

She was ready to give spiritual direction to those who approached her or offer a light-filled word to the receptive. But the primary way she worked, as surely as any missionary, to pass on God was to quietly lead a full spiritual life of prayer, sacraments, and hidden sacrifices. Living deep in divine providence, Elizabeth

---

63 This supranatural energy is seen in some saints.

64 An official Servant of God, her Cause for official sainthood is underway.

developed that foreknowledge that can arise in God's friends: she knew before her death in his arms from breast cancer that Felix—who had never been nagged, only loved—would read her journals, be converted through experiences of divine providence, and become a priest. Until his death in 1950 as a priest in the Dominican order, Father Felix Leseur passed on what Elizabeth, as God's messenger, taught him after her death, about what he identified as "the designs of divine providence."

TWO OR MORE FAITH-FILLED PEOPLE PRAYING TOGETHER

What better example of united prayer than Solanus Casey, that man of boundless faith lived out in service and prayer for others. When it came to prayer, whether involving the men in a soup-kitchen line or someone dying of cancer, in his humility Solanus preferred not to spotlight himself. Instead he liked to connect need for prayer with that of a huge prayer army—the Capuchin Franciscans all over the world. So he often enrolled those in need who were willing and where it was appropriate (for non-Catholics, he proposed other things) in the Seraphic Mass Association (today the Capuchin Mission Mass Association). This required a small enrollment donation (and Solanus was willing to make it very small indeed) that went to support Capuchin work in foreign areas. Solanus had complete confidence that these prayers would produce benefits in whatever form God knew was best.

One day, Solanus had a visit from John McKenna, another man of faith. A worker in the Detroit auto industry, McKenna was enthusiastic about the Seraphic Mass Association and what prayer can do. The industry was in terrible straits and the companies had all shut down for a period that Christmas, then one by one slowly started up with as few as one or two days' work a week for their employees. Chevrolet, where McKenna worked, was one of the worst-off firms. The father of a family poured out his trouble to Solanus: he had not had a full day's work in two weeks. That day he had had only two hours. He couldn't support his family like this. He wanted Chevrolet enrolled in the Seraphic Mass Association.

Solanus thought about it: Masses were said for many worthy causes, including work for those in need. He found no reason not to enroll in the Mass Association the auto company for the prayer power of five hundred Masses said by his fellow Capuchins. It was done. Then priest and layman, two men of faith, praying themselves, waited for divine providence. The official account of Solanus' life, done for his beatification Cause, states, "That same night the company received an astounding order. Two nights later McKenna [visited]: 'Father! We had overtime yesterday and today, and we heard this afternoon that the company has an order for 45,000 machines [cars], wanted in thirty days.'" The book's editor says, "It was believed that order also saved Detroit itself from bankruptcy."

TEACHING THE YOUNG

St. John Bosco, while a great man of prayer and self-sacrifice, was called to pass on his enormous trust in divine providence not just by his remarkable life but also by teaching and mentoring the young. The boys living with Don Bosco and his mother were mostly youths rescued from bad situations. No matter how tired the saint was, at bedtime he gave them all a little "good night" talk that built trust in God. He looked out for each boy individually, too, for one thing making sure the jobs he often got them himself, or the schools where he often paid for them to go—through providence—were not environments that kill faith in divine realities.

Because of Bosco's gift of foreknowledge, certain boys, such as Michael Rua, got special mentoring for roles that Bosco knew, as they did not, lay ahead in their lives. Years later when he had become Bosco's first successor as head of the Salesians, Rua had been tutored in divine providence so well that he too, in moments of need, would find food and Eucharistic Hosts multiply in his hands.

After many failures, Don Bosco also built up a corps of collaborators. These were his Salesian priests and brothers, laypeople called "Cooperators," and thousands of enthusiastic former students of Bosco himself and of his spiritual sons, sent out to create—in partnership with God—other residential havens, playgrounds, and (particularly vocational) schools for boys. In their turn, they taught and modeled divine providence. Bosco died in 1888. The ongoing existence of his Salesians[65] is both a proof of God's providential blessings and passes them on to thousands year after year.

TELLING THE STORIES

Chiara Lubich used stories in talks to people of every faith or none, live, by media, or through her voluminous writings. Always she sought to pass on both what she and her first companions learned, pooling their resources and letting them flow out to any needy person with trust in God's ongoing replenishment, as well as what over the years evolved into philosophies and community lifestyles in "divine providence economics." You will resonate to this story of how, through Chiara and the Focolare, an entire people was saved.

In Cameroon in the first half of the 1960s, a delegation from a remote African animist people, the Bangwa, visited the nearest Catholic bishop, bringing an offering and asking that he seek help for them from the bishop's God. Their tragedy: they were dying as a people, with an infant mortality rate of 85 percent plus four hundred children's deaths in a short period. Having worked with Chiara, the bishop deputized her to help. Chiara had early taken vows of chastity to facilitate her service to others and her total dependence on God. When she traveled to Fontem where the tribe lived in 1966, she had already been looking to providence for every need for over twenty years. She

---

65 There is also a large women's order that the saint co-founded with St. Mary Mazzarello (d. 1881), the Daughters of Mary, Help of Christians, to serve the needs of girls.

met their king (called the Fon), some clan chiefs, and several hundred tribe members. These people laid their needs before her. Chiara, in turn, laid the movement she represented before them. The entire group "got" what Focolare is about. Open, the Bangwa could receive divine providence. As Chiara wrote them years later:

> What was most important was already here. You, my dearest brothers and sisters . . . and most of all, God was here with you, that God to whom you had prayed so earnestly for his help . . . for your children and your beloved families. That day we all felt his presence . . . like a great sun which embraced us all . . . *He gave you the certainty that he would provide for all your needs* [my italics] [and] he gave me and my colleagues the strength and the means to begin to do something.

"Doing something" began right then. Chiara did not tell the tribe she would go back to Europe and try to raise money from the wealthy, write a grant for help from a foundation, or look to some quasi-government body such as UNESCO for assistance. She did not even say she'd appeal to Focolare members. Without any money or personal abilities—such as being a physician— to meet their needs, relying totally on God, she promised this remote, primitive people doctors, health facilities, and schools so their children could live and thrive.

The amazed Bangwa king, the Fon, could not help but say, "You are a woman and therefore nothing, and yet you have accomplished this great work [the Focolare]." Chiara was not offended. As she said, she knew the work was God's; she was just passing on God's abundant supply. (Of course, she also knew how precious she was to God so the slur on her sex by someone who knew no better was more laughable than insulting.)

Over the next years, with the prayer not just of the Focolare and its sympathizers but also, on the initiative of the animist Bangwa—many of them drawn to the faith of the selfless people helping them—their remote area of Cameroon was completely transformed. Through donations from afar and on-the-spot work by volunteers, the second of the Focolare "little cities" was created with a hospital, school, sturdy houses, a hydroelectric station, palm-oil and brick-making industries, and everything else it takes—including a church for the many new followers of Christ—to make a healthy community.

For the rest of her life Chiara liked to pass on the story of this community that demonstrated so well that "God is all-powerful" and "what prayer can obtain" from divine providence.

By now you have stories you can share, too, perhaps some from this book and hopefully personal ones about what God is doing in your life. Be assured that the more you pass them on, the more your own faith will grow and the more divine providence you will see in your life and the lives of those for whom you intercede. Of course, most of us are not going to be able to tell of having made a huge difference in thousands of lives, as the undertakings in economics of the Focolare have done. Let me encourage you not to be concerned about the size or scope of your experiences by what came of a youth's paper-route savings.

The story comes from Millard Fuller (d. 2009), the non-denominational Protestant founder of Habitat for Humanity.

A hugely successful attorney and businessman at an early age, Fuller was spiritually reborn after he gave away everything, when he realized his success and possessions owned him and had brought his marriage to death's door.[66] From then on, he lived, understood, and passed on knowledge of divine providence extraordinarily well (much of it passed on to him from a holy man named Clarence Jordan).[67] Fuller's book *Love in the Mortar Joints*[68] gives all the inspiring details I sum up here:

A young volunteer with Fuller's Habitat for Humanity had saved his paper-route money for years. He would need this $5,000 if he went to medical school. But he didn't need it now. He talked to Millard about what God might want him to do with the money in the meantime rather than leaving it earning interest in the bank.

Millard showed him a letter received that day from a fine man who felt called to accept a low-stipend pastorate on a remote Indian reservation in North Dakota. He was stymied, because if he served in this way, he would not be making enough to pay off $5,000 he had in debts because of the high monthly interest. Somehow he thought he might find help via Fuller.

What played out was as follows: The young man made a no-interest loan through Fuller's ministry to the pastor, who went

---

66 Millard Fuller, *Bokotola* (New Century Publishers, 1977), details his conversion story.

67 Founding Koinonia Farm in 1942 as a "demonstration plot for the Kingdom," this great friend of God's life—struggling against injustice—is one of the endless procession of holy men and women down the centuries in its beauty and power.

68 Millard Fuller and Diane Scott, *Love in the Mortar Joints: The Story of Habitat for Humanity* (Association Press, 1980).

to serve God on the reservation. Every month the pastor made a small payment on the principal. When the youth was ready to start medical school, he needed a certain portion of the money. He contacted Fuller, who checked and found that the little payments had reached exactly that amount. Eventually the entire loan was repaid.

But passing on God's providence didn't end there. The borrower some years later returned from the Indian mission to pastor an Indiana church that, under his leadership, raised thousands of dollars for the ministry, Habitat for Humanity, that had once helped him. The young medical student gave another summer's work to Habitat. All their lives each man would join Millard Fuller in passing on what he learned about God's providence, and how we can be vessels of divine providence for each other if we are open to God and unafraid to listen to the divine voice.

From examining how God met the material needs of saints and other believers and through new experiences of your own, you hopefully now know God's divine providence is real and the sure path through even the most terrible financial and material stresses.

Remember, many others will know this *if* someone reaches out and tells them. Hopefully this chapter has encouraged you to let your life light shine and—whether by prayer and example alone, quietly one-on-one, or from the rooftops, if called—pass on to your sisters and brothers in God's human family that for anyone willing to live in God's friendship, God will provide.

In the end, of course, the prosperity that comes from providence surpasses having a job, money in the bank, health insurance, a paid-off mortgage, fine as these material provisions of providence are. It is living in a prosperity that usually includes but always goes beyond the material. At its apex, it is inhabiting a state some call spiritual maturity, others term emotional-spiritual wholeness, some picture as "living with a foot in this world and the next," and still others describe as saintliness or holiness. Whatever you call it, those of you who early or late attempt (God knows our puny powers) to practice the tenets of this book will have your material needs met and be on the uncrowded road toward riches greater than even the saints can describe.

Pass it on, my dear brothers and sisters. Pass it on.

A REVIEW LIST OF THE NINE WAYS TO POSITION YOURSELF TO RECEIVE DIVINE PROVIDENCE

1. Surrender everything as much as you can.
2. Make serious efforts to grow your faith.
3. Avoid faith-killers like the plague.
4. Cultivate gratitude.
5. Retool your mind.
6. Practice belief in divine providence.
7. Do your part to meet your material needs.
8. Don't block the flow of God's supply.
9. Pass on the wonderful news of God's providence.

ACKNOWLEDGMENTS

My gratitude to Paraclete Press for publishing this book when providence blocked the way at the previous publisher, with special thanks to my very talented final editor Jon Sweeney, and to my unfailingly helpful production editor Sister Mercy Minor and marketing director Sister Madeleine Cleverly, ladies who live up to their combined names, being clever and merciful to a Paraclete newcomer.

My Sophia Institute Press editor Stratford Caldecott, the first to see the project and believe in its value; Sophia publisher John Barger for giving me unfailing encouragement and generously releasing the book for publication elsewhere; Nora Malone, who took on the index and shared the editing with Stratford—each dedicating their considerable talents to improving the work; and my friend Barbara Crowe, with her keen editorial judgment, for reading the manuscript and invaluable suggestions—these four must be thanked heartily for their important contributions. I want to wholeheartedly thank Nora also from the bottom of my heart for her continuing help with technical aspects of the book right up to its publication.

Thanks to one of my spiritual mentors, Father Paul Caporali, SDB, for generously permitting me to quote from his privately published memoir. And to another, Father Jerry Bevilacqua, OSA, for introducing me on retreat to Charles de Foucauld's prayer.

Librarians, archivists, those associated with various saints and saints-in-the making, and other experts have also helped me do my best to see that the material before you is accurate, or have put me in touch with those who could. Some of this help goes back decades. It is impossible to list all who have helped me over the years with my research on the saints I'm writing about in these pages without serious omissions. If you have ever helped me in any way, boundless thanks, and be sure you still have a place in my daily prayers for my benefactors.

For new help during this particular project, my gratitude once again to Capuchin Brothers Leo Wollenweber and Richard Merling of the Father Solanus Guild, Detroit, to EWTN's Thomas Nash, and to Father Bill Delaney, SJ, for more tutoring on Ignatian discernment and help on points of Catholic theology. My appreciation also to Salesian Father Michael Mendl of New Rochelle; Carmelite Father James Geoghagen of San Jose; Brittany Marie Harrison of the Salesian Sisters; Joanne Loewy of New York's Louis Armstrong Center for Music and Medicine at Beth Israel Medical Center and Concetta Tomaino of New York's Beth Abraham Hospital's Institute for Music and Neurological Function; and Focolare members Mary Cass and *Living City* editor Clare Zanzucchi. Thanks to Madonna House in Combermere, Ontario, Canada, for their wonderful books on the Dohertys. Thanks also to University of Portland Wilson W. Clark Memorial Library reference/instruction librarian Stephanie Michel, Sisters of the Blessed Sacrament Archivist Dr. Stephanie Morris, and the staff of Mt. Angel Abbey Library for the generous extended loan of materials on three saints. For another extended loan, heartfelt thanks to my valued good neighbor Mike Munson. I owe a bushel of loving thanks to my daughter Katherine Wilson and my friends Kathy and Mike Sheahan for a host of practical helps, from errands to the technical, that brought these pages to you sooner. That includes gratitude to my daughter for giving time she didn't have to the project's footnotes. Loving gratitude also to my daughter-in-law Jennifer for her gift of a website and to her and my son Christopher for helps with Facebook and other avenues to pass on the message of this and my other books of God's reality, power, and love as seen in the saints of modern times. Profound thanks to my friend Francis Levy, who, amidst intense labors on his second, more extensive biography of Father Aloysius Ellacuria, once again made time to advise me on computer issues and to back up from afar, sometimes several times daily, my progressing work.

Last, loving thanks to other authors and friends who contributed to these pages: Rolf Gompertz, Ronda Chervin, Joan Englander, Father Martinus Cawley, OCSO, and Bert Ghezzi. I would also like to thank Bert for his help with my Scripture references. And, of course, as always I think of you who uphold this writer and work in your prayers. You know who you are. I hope you know the depths of my gratitude as well.

SOURCES ON THE SAINTS

Persons listed here are alphabetized by first name.

(BL.) ALEXANDRINA DA COSTA

Francis Johnston, *Alexandrina: The Agony and the Glory* (TAN Books, 1979). Johnston, a good researcher, worked with and received material from the Salesian who was her spiritual director. I have also revisited my writing on her in *The Sanctified Body* (Doubleday, 1989).

(FATHER) ALOYSIUS ELLACURIA, CMF

Numerous videotaped interviews over the years of those who knew him furnished by their maker, Francis X. Levy, as well as interviews I have done for previous books. Books by three of his close associates: Francis X. Levy's *Our Guide*, Jim Buehner's *Our Living Tabernacle: Fr. Aloysius Ellacuria*, and Father Charles Carpenter's *The Life of Father Aloysius*. All privately published.

(ST.) (BROTHER) ANDRÉ BESSETTE

The author's research and writings in several books on healer Brother André over the past three decades rests on French-language sources, the most significant [out of print], Étienne Catta's monumental work *Le Frère André (1845–1937) et L'Oratoire Saint-Joseph Du Mont-Royal* (Fides), furnished by St. Joseph's, Mt. Royal, Montreal, Canada, where the Holy Cross brother lived and worked.

186186 186 186 186 186 ⮂186 ⮂ GOD WILL PROVIDE186 ⮂ GOD WILL PROVIDE
186 ⮂ GOD WILL PROVIDE

(MOTHER) ANGELICA (RITA RIZZO)

Besides my attendance at her talks and discussions at EWTN, I have used the book by Raymond Arroyo cited in footnote #53 and John Catoir's book in footnote #18.

(BL.) (BROTHER) ARTEMIDES ZATTI, SDB

Booklets: Father Peter Lappin, SDB, *Zatti* (Salesiana Publications, 1987), and Brittany Marie Harrison, Salesian Cooperator, *All Things to All: A Brief Sketch of the Life of Blessed Brother Artemides Zatti* (Salesian Missions, New Rochelle, NY undated).

ADRIENNE VON SPEYR

My Early Years (Ignatius Press, 1995).

(ST.) BAKHITA (MOTHER JOSEPHINE) OF THE CANOSSIAN SISTERS

Her background information taken from the August 15, 2009, letter by Dom Antoine Marie Beauchef, l'Abbaye Saint-Joseph de Clairval, France. In earlier writings, I used a source I can no longer find.

BETSIE TEN BOOM

I have relied on her sister's books for the portrait of Betsie, whose holiness is confirmed in her few written words in *Prison Letters*, its authorship credited to Corrie Ten Boom. See that entry.

CARYLL HOUSELANDER

Caryll's autobiographical *A Rocking Horse Catholic* and her friend and publisher Maisie Ward's biography *That Divine Eccentric*, both out of print. See also footnote #35.

(SERVANT OF GOD) CATHERINE DE HUECK DOHERTY

Among Catherine's twenty-three books published by the community she founded, Madonna House, are a lot of autobiographical writings, and I have used those in preference to writings about her by others, except for writings by her husband (listed under his name) and by Father Émile Brière, the priest who was with her for many years and in whose arms she died. Brière wrote the quote on their marriage in *Katia: A Personal Vision of Catherine de Hueck Doherty* (Éditions Paulines, 1988), 97. For the incident with the coal from Catherine's writings, see footnote #20.

(BL.) (VICOMTE) CHARLES DE FOUCAULD/CHARLES OF JESUS

Used here: Jean-Jacques Antier, *Charles de Foucauld* (Ignatius Press, 1999), 22, 102, 100, 164, 165, and 188; Dom Antoine Marie's untitled article dated January 25, 2006, from Abbaye Saint-Joseph de Clairval; *Spiritual Autobiography of Charles de Foucauld*, ed. and annotated by Jean-François Six (Dimension Books, 1964); and Rene Voillaume (Prior General of the Little Brothers of Jesus, a group that claims Charles as their spiritual founder), *Seeds of the Desert: The Legacy of Charles de Foucauld* (Anthony Clarke, 1972).

CHARLES RICH

Ronda Chervin, ed., *The Holy Dybbuk: Letters of Charles Rich, Contemplative* (St. Bede's Publications, 1988). I have also read his online biography by Chervin: www.friendsofCharlesRich.com.

CHIARA LUBICH (SILVIA LUBICH)

Chiara Lubich: A Life for Unity: An Interview by Franca Zambonini (Edizioni Paoline, 1991; New City, 1992); and vol. 47, no. 5/6 of *Living City* (an American Focolare-published magazine), the special edition on Chiara published immediately following her death on March 14, 2008. The story of the Bangwa new city Fontem: Jim Gallagher, *A Woman's Work: Chiara Lubich: A Biography of the Focolare Movement and Its Founder* (New City, 1997). Duccia's testimony from the interview with her by Mario Dal Bello, *Living City* (December 1995): 18–22. Regarding Chiara's friendship with Pope John Paul II: *Living City* (April/May 2011): 33.

CORRIE TEN BOOM

Her three books: *The Hiding Place*, with John and Elizabeth Sherrill (Chosen Books, 1971)(pp. 30–31 for Corrie's conversation with her father about "sex sin"); *Prison Letters* (Fleming H. Revell, 1975; Bantam, 1978); *Tramp for the Lord*, with Jamie Buckingham (Fleming H. Revell, 1974).

(SERVANT OF GOD) DOROTHY DAY

Robert Coles, *Dorothy Day: A Radical Devotion* (Radcliffe Biography Series: Da Capo Press, 1987), for Cole's interviews of her. The comments by Dorothy's father are in William D.

Miller, *Dorothy Day: A Biography* (Harper and Row Publishers, 1982), 311, cited by the editor of her diaries, p 41, footnote #47: Robert Ellsberg, ed., *The Duty of Delight* (Marquette University Press, 2008). *The Long Loneliness: An Autobiography* (Harper and Row, 1952).

(FATHER) EDDIE DOHERTY

The autobiographical book *Gall and Honey* (Madonna House, 1989), on his first two marriages and career; *Tumbleweed: A Biography* of his third wife Catherine de Hueck Doherty (Madonna House, 198) and *A Cricket in My Heart* (Blue House Press, 1990) on his life with Catherine. On his marriage to Catherine, see also her entry for their priest friend's assessment of the relationship.

(SISTER) ELENA AIELLO

Francesco Spadafora, *The Incredible Life Story of Sister Elena Aiello: The Calabrian Holy Nun (1895–1961)*, trans. Angelo R. Cioffi (Theo. Gaus' Sons, 1964), furnished to me by Sister of Charity Jeannette Humes, Southwest Regional Minister of her order.

(SERVANT OF GOD) ELIZABETH LESEUR

Elizabeth Leseur, *My Spirit Rejoices* (Sophia Institute Press, 1996), and *Light in the Darkness: How to Bring Christ to the Souls You Meet Each Day* (Sophia Institute Press, 1998), relying especially on the introduction by her husband, Felix.

(BL.) ELIZABETH OF THE TRINITY

Thomas Larkin, OCD, *Elizabeth of the Trinity: Her Life and Spirituality* (Carmelite Centre of Spirituality, 1984); Conrad De Meester and John Sullivan, *Light Love Life: A Look at a Face and a Heart* (ICS Publications, 1987); and Hans Urs von Balthasar, *Two Sisters in the Spirit: Thérèse of Lisieux and Elizabeth of the Trinity* (Ignatius Press, 1992).

EVE LAVALLIÈRE (ÉUGENIE FENOGLIO)

Boniface Hanley, OFM, *No Strangers to Violence, No Strangers to Love* (Ave Maria Press, 1983).

(ST.) FRANCES (FRANCESCA IN ITALIAN) CABRINI

Footnote #24 for the best Cabrini biography, written by the saint's companion, Mother Saverio De Maria. I have reviewed my *The Sanctified Body* (Doubleday, 1989) for some of the mystical phenomena associated with this saint.

(BL.) (FATHER) FRANCIS XAVIER SEELOS

My interviews with her on Father Seelos' role in Angela Boudreaux's life are in my (currently being updated) *Nothing Short of a Miracle* (Doubleday, 1989; Our Sunday Visitor, 1995). My writings on Seelos are based on interviews with Angela and other individuals, as well as biographies, videos, and other materials furnished me by my friend the late Redemptorist Father Joseph Elworthy at the saint's New Orleans shrine, and the helpful current director Father Byron Miller, CSSR.

(ST.) GABRIEL POSSENTI

Gabriele Cingolani, CP, *Saint Gabriel Possenti, Passionist: A Young Man in Love,* trans. S. B. Zak (Alba House, 1997). This book by a member of the Passionists is so good I no longer use any other biography.

(ST.) GASPARE (OR CASPER) DEL BUFALO

Father William A. Volk of the Missionaries of the Most Precious Blood (also known as the Congregation of the Most Precious Blood), the order founded by del Bufalo, furnished me with the two-volume biography by A. Rey and a biography by Giuseppe De Libero, both in Italian. It is from these that I have taken the incidents described on p. 73. In English translation: *Gaspar del Bufalo* by Monsignor Vincent Sardi (Messenger Press, 1954). See also my book *The Sanctified Body*.

GEORGE MÜLLER

Roger Steer, *George Müller: Delighted in God!* (Harold Shaw Publishers, 1981).

(ST.) (DR.) GIANNA BERETTA MOLLA

See her photos in most biographies, including on the cover of *A Woman's Life—Saint Gianna Beretta Molla* and *Saint Gianna Molla: Wife, Mother, Doctor,* and two others found at www.CatholicCompany.com.

(PÈRE) JACQUES BUNEL, OCD

At Bunel's Carmel in Avon, France, I was directed to excellent biographies and other materials in French by the late Père

Jean-Marie Petitétienne, OCD. In English: *Père Jacques* by Michel Carrouges (Macmillan, 1961) and *Resplendent in Victory* by Francis J. Murphy (ICS Publications, 1998).

(SERVANT OF GOD) JAN TYRANOWSKI

See listing under Pope John Paul II.

(ST.) JEAN MARIE VIANNEY (THE CURÉ D'ARS)

I still use and prefer Dom Ernest Graf's (out of print) translation of Abbé Francis Trochu's *The Cure d'Ars*, done "according to the Acts of the Process of Canonization and numerous hitherto unpublished documents" (Newman Press, 1960).

(ST.) (DON) JOHN BOSCO

Already during his lifetime those who lived with Don Bosco were keeping records of things the saint said and did. Much of this material, such as Joseph Brosio's testimony (footnote #56), was collected in the nineteen-volume *Biographical Memoirs of St. John Bosco.* Of my many biographies on this saint, I also consulted a favorite (out of print), Salesian A. Auffray's *Saint John Bosco* ([England's] Salesian Publications, 1930), 111, regarding Don Bosco and the stress of the church project in Rome.

(ST) JOHN NEUMANN, CSSR

Rev. Michael J. Curley, CSSR (a member of Neumann's order with access to all the original materials), *Bishop John Neumann, CSSR: A Biography* (Bishop Neumann Center, 1952). His mother's aversion to gossip is on p. 5.

(BL.) (POPE) JOHN XXIII (ANGELO GIUSEPPE RONCALLI)

My book *Meet John XXIII: Joyful Pope and Father to All* (Servant Press, 2008) gives details of my four years of research, most importantly interviews with John's private secretary and literary executor, retired Archbishop Loris F. Capovilla, and the materials he made available, in Italian or French. Regarding the friendship of Popes John and Paul VI, this relationship was shared with me by Capovilla, who worked with both men and collected and published their letters, *Giovanni e Paolo: Due Papi: Saggio di Corrispondenza, 1925–62* (Studium, 1982). I have translated and quoted from Capovilla's preface to that book and also used unsigned material at its front.

(BL.) (POPE) JOHN PAUL II (KAROL WOJTYLA)

For background information, I have consulted several books on John Paul by his private secretary (later Archbishop) Stanislaw Dziwis and by his close associate Joseph Cardinal Ratzinger (Pope Benedict XVI). Among my biographies by professional writers, I used the well-researched and detailed book done during the pope's life by American George Weigel, *Witness to Hope: The Biography of Pope John Paul II* (HarperCollins, 1999). On John Paul II's friendship with Mother Teresa, see brief references to their mutual esteem in Kathryn Spink's early work on Mother Teresa, *The Miracle of Love* (HarperCollins, 1982), and many more references in Spink's later *Mother Teresa: A Complete Authorized Biography* (Harper, 1997) of "a relationship of reciprocal personal respect and affection" (p. 178), with examples. I find most moving their exchange of messages when she is felled with

194   GOD WILL PROVIDE

a heart blockage—his full of warm concern and prayer, hers to assure him "I am offering it all for you" (p. 222). Two references to the relationship are found in Mother Teresa's own writings, *Come Be My Light* (see her entry below), and the friendship is also mentioned by Weigel (see his book's index). On John Paul's formative relationship with Jan Tyranowski, see Weigel's index.

(ST.) JOSEPH CAFASSO

St. John Bosco's *St. Joseph Cafasso: Priest of the Gallows* (TAN, 1983).

(ST.) JOSEPH COTTOLENGO

His three-volume life in Italian supposedly exists in an abridged English version. I've never found it. All I know about this giant of providence is found in books on his contemporaries, such as St. John Bosco, and simple sources, such as Butler's four-volume *Lives of the Saints*, April 29th entry.

(ST.) (MOTHER) KATHARINE DREXEL AND HER PARENTS

Sisters of the Blessed Sacrament Archivist Dr. Stephanie Morris has been a main source. I used Blessed Sacrament Sister Consuela Marie Duffy's *Katharine Drexel: A Biography*, published in 1966 by the guild that promoted her Cause, and a quick summary biography with photographs, the booklet *A Philadelphia Story* by Boniface Hanley, OFM, also published by the guild, that first appeared in the magazine *The Anthonian* in 1984 (first quarter issue).

(BL.) LAURA VICUNA

I have Laura's story in a number of Salesian publications, including the biography by Rev. Paul Aronica, SDB, *Rose of the Andes* (Salesiana, 1957). It is the Salesians women's order Daughters of Mary, Help of Christians, who educated Laura and, with the men's order, after her death, carried forward her Cause.

(SERVANT OF GOD) LÉONIE MARTIN (SISTER FRANÇOISE THÉRÈSE)

Materials used by this author are in French from my work in Lisieux when I also stayed overnight at Léonie's Visitation monastery in Caen. One of these has been translated into English: Marie Baudouin, *A Difficult Life*, trans. Mary Frances Mooney (Veritas Publications, 1993). I have also found her story over and over in biographies of her canonized sister, of the Martin family, and—as it was unfolding during Zélie's lifetime—her mother's letters. See Zélie Martin. I used also a fine several-page biography by Dom Antoine Marie of the French Benedictine Abbey of St. Joseph de Clairval available at http://www.thereseoflisieux.org/leonie-martin-letter-from-clai/ and a more detailed one by Sister Mary Christine Martens, VHM, in three parts at http://www.helpfellowship.org/Sr_Françoise-Thérèse.htm.

(BL.) LOUIS MARTIN

His daughter Céline's biography, *The Father of the Little Flower: Louis Martin (1823–94)* (TAN, 2005), also contains some of his letters. The other four daughters' memories I found in their memoirs or in books about each one, particularly Thérèse's *Story of a Soul.* I used also Stéphane-Joseph Piat, *The Story of a Family* (P.J. Kenedy and Sons, 1947), and Dr. Joyce R. Emert, OCDS, *Louis Martin: Father of a Saint* (Alba House, 1983). Regarding his and Zélie's full collection of letters, see her listing.

MARTHE ROBIN

My sources are French biographies by (Rev.) Raymond Peyret and by Jean Guitton. Find Peyret's in English as *The Cross and the Joy* (Alba House, 1983). I am also indebted to the Foyers de Charité founded by Marthe for material during earlier writings on her.

(ST.) MARY MACKILLOP

Lesley O'Brien, *Mary Mackillop Unveiled* (HarperCollins, 1994), furnished me by the saint's order. For this book and my article on Mary for *Word Among Us* I have also used the Postulator's biography: Paul Gardiner, SJ, *An Extraordinary Australian: Mary McKillop* (E.J. Dwyer PTY Limited / David Ell Press, 1994).

(BL.) MARY OF PROVIDENCE (EUGÉNIE SMET)

Marie C. Buehrle, *I Am on Fire: Blessed Mary of Providence* (Catholic Life Publications, 1963), and Marie Rene-Bazin, *She Who Lived Her Name: Mary of Providence* (Mercier Press Limited, 1948).

(ST.) MAXÍMILIAN KOLBE

See my biography *A Man for Others* (Harper and Row, 1982) presently in paperback: www.MarytownPress.com. Based on my interviews or first-person witnesses, this biography gives the testimonies of roughly one hundred people who knew Kolbe over his lifetime, including the witnesses I cite in these pages. They are named there.

(ST.) MICHAEL RUA

I use the reliable books by his fellow Salesians: John Ayers, SDB, *Blessed Michael Rua* (Saint Paul Publications, 1974), and Peter Lappin, *The Wine in the Chalice* (Salelsiana, 1972), but I also turned for Rua's earlier life to my materials on his mentor, St. John Bosco.

MILLARD FULLER

Material used in this book is taken from chapter 8 of his *Love in the Mortar Joints* (New Wine Publishing, 1980). I have also reviewed the story of his founding of Habitat for Humanity, in Fuller's book *Boktola* (New Century Publishers, 1977) and accessed his obituary online.

(POPE) PAUL VI

See Listing Under John XXIII.

(BL.) PIER GIORGIO FRASSATI

His sister Luciana Frassati's *Man of the Beatitudes* (St. Paul Publications, 1990). I also reviewed materials at the website of Frassati USA, Inc. (www.frassatiusa.org).

(VENERABLE) PIERRE TOUSSAINT

I have used the best book, available only in French to date. Rich in detail and filled with the saint's own letters, it was given to me by its creator, my Haitian benefactor Salesian Père Maurice E. Hyppolite. Père Hyppolite has translated into French a book written originally in English that was finished just at Ven. Pierre's death in 1853 by Hannah Farnham Sawyer Lee (d. 1865), one of Toussaint's many white friends. A second book on the saint, mixing the life with meditations by Father Hyppolite, is also still available only in French.

(ST.) (PADRE) PIO OF PIETRELCINA (FRANCESCO FORGIONE)

I refer back to my three books *Meet Padre Pio: Beloved Mystic, Miracle-Worker and Spiritual Guide; Quiet Moments with Padre Pio;* and *Through the Year with Padre Pio,* each done with materials either supplied by the saint's Our Lady of Grace Friary or recommended by the late Father Joseph Pius Martin of that friary, spiritual son of the saint and one of Padre Pio's caregivers. Since Father Joseph Pius' death, authentic materials have come to me from Charles Abercrombie at Our Lady of Grace Friary. I have also gone back to the English-language biography I bought, at Fr. Joseph Pius Martin's recommendation, when visiting him at Pio's friary: *Padre Pio of Pietrelcina: "Everybody's Cyrenean"* (1996). And I reread portions of the popular American biography in its revised, expanded edition of Bernard Ruffin, *Padre Pio: The True Story* (Our Sunday Visitor, 1991). See pp. 282–86 in Ruffin's book for the building of Pio's hospital.

RHODA WISE

The Ohio mystic's story can be found in my book *Messengers: After-Death Appearances of Saints and Mystics* (OSV, 1995) done from material supplied by Catholic Church authorities in Ohio. Rhoda's story has been cut from the condensed paperback version retitled *Apparitions of Modern Saints* (Servant, 2001).

RONDA CHERVIN

Chervin, a friend of the author's, has also shared with me about the good her spiritual friendship with contemplative Charles Rich did her. For written references to that relationship and her comments on friendships rooted in God, see Chervin's introduction to the collection of his letters to her that she edited under the listing for Charles Rich. Information on this topic is also in Chervin's autobiography: *Enroute to Eternity: The Story of My Life* (Miriam Press, 1994).

(VEN.) (FATHER) SOLANUS CASEY, OFM, CAP

I have used the Postulation Biography: Michael Crosby, OFM, CAP, ed., *Solanus Casey: The Official Account of a Virtuous American Life* (Crossroad Publishing Company, 2000). Note particularly pp. 79–80 for Father Solanus' written testimony on "Saving Detroit," that he did not ascribe to his own prayers; p. 93 for part of the account by Father Hermann Buss on the miracle described in this book's prologue; pp. 122–23 about asking people to do something for God that would help them know him better and about redemptive suffering; p. 143 about his gratitude on his deathbed; and p. 202 about the healing of the man who hadn't been to church since his wedding. For an analysis of Solanus' personality and inner life, I have used Father Crosby's earlier biography: *Thank God Ahead of Time: The Life and Spirituality of Solanus Casey* (Franciscan Herald Press, 1985). See p. 142–44 about his gratitude in pain and illness. Thirdly, I re-read Brother Leo Wollenweber, OFM, CAP, *Meet Solanus Casey: Spiritual Counselor and Wonder Worker* (Servant Press, 2002). Saintly Brother Leo worked with Father Solanus and writes, as none of the others can, from his long-term personal observations of Father Solanus. Finally, I revisited James Patrick Derum, *The Porter of Saint Bonaventure's: The Life of Father Solanus Casey, Capuchin* (Fidelity Press, 1968). The first biography, it has the advantage of interviews with many people who knew Solanus, including his blood brother. I also turn to my own book on God's healing power in modern saints, *Nothing Short of a Miracle* (updated version forthcoming), for its sketch of the saint's life in relation to his healing charism. For the prologue's official testimony on the "miraculous" arrival of provisions at the Detroit soup kitchen see footnote #2.

(BL.) TERESA OF CALCUTTA

From the many books I've read for background, all by people who worked closely with Teresa, I used here only the two by Kathryn Spink (see the entry for John Paul II—where their friendship is discussed—for titles and publishing detail) and Teresa's own writings edited and with commentary by Brian Kolodiejchuk, who knew her for twenty years, is the Postulator of her Cause, and a priest member of the men's branch of her order. See footnote #14 for publication details and regarding the saint's foray for food during Hindu-Muslim conflict. See footnote #15 regarding my sources for Mother Teresa's lovers "battle" with Jesus before she founded the Missionaries.

(SERVANT OF GOD) THERESA NEUMANN

Mystical Phenomena in the Life of Theresa Neuman by Most Rev. Josef Teodorowicz, Archbishop of Lemberg (B. Herder Book Company, 1940), and Johannes Steiner, *Thérèse Neumann* (Alba House, 1967). These are each authoritative sources by writers who knew Theresa, did thorough investigating, and were given access to the documentation and the witnesses of her charisms and life, which they also saw personally. Both books originally appeared in German. I have others, but these give all one needs.

(ST.) THÉRÈSE OF LISIEUX (THÉRÈSE MARTIN)

I have used my favorite English-language version of her autobiography, John Beevers, *Story of a Soul* (Image, 1957), and Beevers' biographies *Storm of Glory: The Story of St. Thérèse of Lisieux* (Image Books, 1955) and *Saint Thérèse, The Little Flower: The Making of a Saint* (TAN, 1976); *St. Thérèse: Her Last Conversations*, trans. John Clarke, OCD (ICS Publications, 1977); *St. Thérèse of Lisieux by Those Who Knew Her: Testimonies from the Process of Beatification*, ed. and trans. Christopher O'Mahoney, OCD (Our Sunday Visitor, 1975); Sister Geneviève of the Holy Face (Céline Martin), *My Sister Saint Thérèse* (TAN, 1997); and Conrad De Meester, OCD, ed., *Saint Thérèse of Lisieux: Her Life,*

Times, and Teaching (ICS Publications, 1997). Regarding her worldwide work as co-Patron of the missions, I refer to my own book, done from work in the archives of her Carmel in Lisieux, *Messengers: After-Death Appearances of Saints and Mystics,* or its paperback published as *Apparitions of Saints and Mystics* (details under Rhoda Wise).

(BL.) (FATHER) TITUS BRANDSMA, OCARM

I used *A Heart on Fire,* a thick booklet by a fellow Carmelite Fr. Albert Groeneveld ([England's] Carmelite Press, 1979) I found researching at the saint's archives in Nijmegen, Holland. I also consulted Joseph Rees, *Titus Brandsma: A Modern Martyr* (Sidgwick and Jackson, 1971), and the chapter in Boniface Hanley, *No Strangers to Violence, No Strangers to Love* (Ave Maria Press, 1995).

(BL.) ZÉLIE GUERIN MARTIN

Zélie is best known through her delightful, down-to-earth letters that I have in French as *Zélie et Louis Martin: Correspondance Familiale (1863–85)* (Les Éditions du Cerf, 2004). They are newly available in English as *A Call to a Deeper Love: The Family Correspondence of the Parents of St. Thérèse of the Child Jesus, Blessed Zélie and Louis Martin* (Alba House, 2011). For context I use *The Story of a Family* by Stéphane-Joseph Piat (P.J. Kenedy and Sons, 1947); her daughter Thérèse's autobiography (see her listing); and the various translated biographies of her daughters, Marie, Pauline, Léonie, Céline, and Thérèse, or her husband, Louis Martin (see his listing).

INDEX OF NAMES

ABOUT PARACLETE PRESS

WHO WE ARE

Paraclete Press is a publisher of books, recordings, and DVDs on Christian spirituality. Our publishing represents a full expression of Christian belief and practice—from Catholic to Evangelical, from Protestant to Orthodox.

We are the publishing arm of the Community of Jesus, an ecumenical monastic community in the Benedictine tradition. As such, we are uniquely positioned in the marketplace without connection to a large corporation and with informal relationships to many branches and denominations of faith.

WHAT WE ARE DOING

Books | Paraclete publishes books that show the richness and depth of what it means to be Christian. Although Benedictine spirituality is at the heart of all that we do, we publish books that reflect the Christian experience across many cultures, time periods, and houses of worship. We publish books that nourish the vibrant life of the church and its people—books about spiritual practice, formation, history, ideas, and customs.

We have several different series, including the best-selling Paraclete Essentials and Paraclete Giants series of classic texts in contemporary English; A Voice from the Monastery—men and women monastics writing about living a spiritual life today; award-winning poetry; best-selling gift books for children on the occasions of baptism and first communion; and the Active Prayer Series that brings creativity and liveliness to any life of prayer.

Recordings | From Gregorian chant to contemporary American choral works, our music recordings celebrate sacred choral music through the centuries. Paraclete distributes the recordings of the internationally acclaimed choir Gloriæ Dei Cantores, praised for their "rapt and fathomless spiritual intensity" by *American Record Guide*, and the Gloriæ Dei Cantores Schola, which specializes in the study and performance of Gregorian chant. Paraclete is also the exclusive North American distributor of the recordings of the Monastic Choir of St. Peter's Abbey in Solesmes, France, long considered to be a leading authority on Gregorian chant.

Videos | Our videos offer spiritual help, healing, and biblical guidance for life issues: grief and loss, marriage, forgiveness, anger management, facing death, and spiritual formation.

Learn more about us at our website:
www.paracletepress.com,
or call us toll-free at 1-800-451-5006.

SCAN
TO
READ
MORE

YOU MAY ALSO BE INTERESTED IN . . .

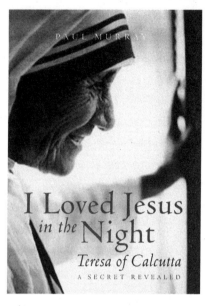

I Loved Jesus in the Night

Paul Murray

$19.95
Hardcover
ISBN: 978-1-55725-579-2

"To be in love and yet not to love, to live by faith and yet not to believe. To spend myself and yet to be in total darkness."

—Teresa of Calcutta

I Loved Jesus in the Night is one priest's compelling account of meeting the saint of Calcutta. Sharing anecdotes and firsthand experiences, Paul Murray offers a glimpse into why Mother Teresa could declare in one of her letters that if ever she were to "become a saint," she would surely be one of "darkness." These intimate reflections on her "private writings" illumine the meaning of a life that is only now beginning to be understood.

Paul Murray, OP, is an Irish Dominican, poet, and professor in Rome at the University of St. Thomas, the "Angelicum."

Words of Light
Inspiration from the Letters of Padre Pio

Compiled and with an Introduction by
Fr. Raniero Cantalamessa

$14.99
Paperback
ISBN: 978-1-55725-643-0

"[In these letters] I quickly discovered the same states of soul that were described by the great mystics. Padre Pio's own 'dark night' was in no way inferior to that described by John of the Cross; and equally the 'living flame' of his love for God dazzles the reader and allows them to catch a glimpse of another world."

—Fr. Raniero Cantalamessa,
Preacher to the Papal Household,
from the book's Introduction

Available from most booksellers or through Paraclete Press:
www.paracletepress.com; 1-800-451-5006.
Try your local bookstore first.